Arch, Steeples, and Dome

Religious Symbols on a Journey of Faith

To Jeane with many good wishes and

A Reflective Memoir
by
Marie Kevin Tighe, S.P.
2009

authorHOUSE®

AuthorHouse™
1663 Liberty Drive, Suite 200
Bloomington, IN 47403
www.authorhouse.com
Phone: 1-800-839-8640

© 2009 Marie Kevin Tighe, S.P.. All rights reserved.

No part of this book may be reproduced, stored in a retrieval system, or transmitted by any means without the written permission of the author.

First published by AuthorHouse 10/9/2009

ISBN: 978-1-4389-9602-8 (e)
ISBN: 978-1-4389-9601-1 (sc)

Printed in the United States of America
Bloomington, Indiana

This book is printed on acid-free paper.

Arch, Steeples, and Dome
Religious Symbols on a Journey of Faith
1972-2006

Introduction	vii

Prologue
1924-1962	My Life Before the Council	xi
1962-1965	The Second Vatican Council: An Overview	xxii
1965-1972 -	Years Immediately Following the Council	xxvii

Part I. The Arch (1972-1980)
A. A New Frontier	3
B. Two Prophets	12
C. Individual and Corporate Renewal	17
D. Trends, Values, Norms, Climate, and a Process Approach to Change	23
E. The Spirituality of Groups	32

Part II. Steeples (1980-1992)
A. Reaching for God	37
B. Structures - A Means of Growth and Renewal	42
C. Bringing Structures to Life	49
D. Widening Circles of Church	58
E. Called to Be the Church in a New Way	62

Part III. Lighthouse Interlude (1992-1996)

Part IV. Dome (1996-2006)
A. The Purpose of the Church	75
B. A Universal Home	79
C. Woman of the Church	85
D. Celebrating with the World	90

Epilogue	99
Endnotes	101
Suggested References and Readings	104
Acknowledgements	107

INTRODUCTION
Why this book? ... Why now?

We are now more than forty years beyond the closing of the Second Vatican Council. The powerful and challenging documents issuing from that Council as official Church teachings have yet to be fully understood, absorbed, and implemented. This personal and reflective memoir is simply an account of one effort to assist religious communities and other ecclesiastical units, to begin or to continue, the process of understanding, absorbing, and implementing the call of the Council.

Hopefully, this book will appear not too far behind two scholarly works, which address the same concern. One is, Vatican II: Did Anything Happen? [1] and the other one, What Happened at Vatican II? [2]. The appearance of these two books as I began to write this one, confirmed my belief that, as a Church, we are not justified in moving on in time without a serious examination of our fidelity to the teachings of the most recent formal Council of the Universal Church. The questions in those two titles, coming as they do at this point in the new millennium, are both courageous and challenging!

In an article, "The Shape of the Church to Come,"[3] Timothy Radcliffe, O.P. offers these wise words leading to a clear focus question. "The shape of the church to come will also be determined by how it interacts with the world. The Church faces the dilemma that has shaped Judaism over the centuries: how to avoid both assimilation to society, which would lead to the church's disappearance, and the ghetto, another form of death. What sort of dynamic interaction with the world would let the church flourish?"

So the "Why?" and the "Why now?" of this book lie in what seems to me to be an urgency to address, even at this late date, the call of the Second Vatican Council to intensify our efforts to be recognized as the Church, the Mystical Body of Christ, in our time. Otherwise, we will lose the power of attracting new members and the growing number of former members will escalate, both in the Church at large, and in religious communities in particular.

Prologue

1924-1962   My Life Before
            the Council

1962-1965   The Second
            Vatican Council:
            An Overview

1965-1972   Years Immediately
            Following the
            Council

Prologue
1924-1962   *My Life Before the Council*

While this is not an autobiography, it may be helpful to readers to know something about my early personal and family backgrounds before we move into the major topics of this memoir. In this part of the prologue I will also share some of the significant aspects of my first twenty years as a Sister of Providence of Saint Mary-of-the-Woods, Indiana. This will provide insights into the theology and rationale for many of the changes in congregations of apostolic women religious. With that said, let us step back about eighty-five years.

I was born on August 23, 1924, in one of the southernmost towns of Indiana, along the Ohio River. New Albany, Indiana is directly across the Ohio River from Louisville, Kentucky. I was the seventh child and sixth daughter of Edward J. Tighe and Anna Buche Tighe. The first child and only boy died in infancy. His name was Paul Edward Tighe, making his initials "P.E.T." A friend of my mother had given her a small silver cup with those initials engraved on it. That cup was always in the front and center of our dining room dish cabinet. Each April 5th, on Paul's birthday, my father would wait for a rare lull in the conversation of his six daughters during the evening meal. He would say simply, "Well, today is Paul's birthday." There would be a moment of silence. It was an annual ritual during which my father and mother remembered their only begotten son. It was a kind of family reunion.

Even though I was the last girl to be born, I had the honor of receiving my mother's name, Anna Therese. I remember hearing that my father said to my mother at the time, "I think that after six girls we could surely name one for you." I received that name at my baptism the day after I was born. Later that name held a second sacred significance for me when I learned that it was also the baptismal name of Saint Mother Theodore, the foundress of the Sisters of Providence in America. Many years later Saint Mother Theodore would become a second mother for me.

Having five older sisters kept me on the straight and narrow path, but that was done in a loving and caring way. My childhood spanned the time between two world wars, and was touched by the depression of the late twenties and early thirties. In spite of that fact, our home life was free of great distress because of a simple lifestyle, and the careful and responsible planning of both of our parents. I grew up literally in the shadow of Holy Trinity Church where all of us were baptized into the Catholic faith. One block away there was another Catholic church, Saint Mary's. When my parents were married, all of the sermons at Saint Mary's were still being delivered in German. That had been my mother's parish as she was of German descent. My father was of Irish descent and did not understand German, so Holy Trinity became our family's parish. Ours was a blend of Irish and German heritage, which, I have been told, is a good blend. By simple childhood observation I can attest to that, having never experienced a single time of disagreement nor argumentation between my parents. Rather, one of my earliest memories is that of watching my parents waltzing in the living room and experiencing their joy in each other's presence. I have to admit that as the youngest in the family I had a privileged childhood. This period in American cultural life contributed greatly to that, also. The pace of life was slower and family life, in general, was more centered in the home. Long before we heard the Second Vatican Council refer to the family as the "domestic church," I was being grounded in the community dimension of the Church in my own family life. There were many people to look after me and to be interested in my general well-being, I truly believe that my earliest memory as a young child was that of kneeling beside the bathtub and being taught my first prayers by my second oldest sister, Edith.

The prayers were, "Baby Jesus, meek and mild, make my heart your cradle." and "Jesus make me just like Mary; Mary keep me just like you." Those were prayers a child could understand. As I grew older in the faith I realized how much they were at the core of Christian spirituality. The first prayer was for union with Jesus and the second prayer was one of petition for likeness to Jesus' sinless mother.

Along with my nourishment in the spiritual life, the family showed an interest in my favorite sports. My involvement with tennis, basketball, and baseball made up for the lack of a brother, but only in that one respect. As a family we did not have extravagant vacations. My one bachelor uncle was co-owner of Scout Mountain Lodge on Blue River about thirty miles from New Albany. Each summer my family spent two weeks there hiking, swimming, and boating. That was as much a family highlight as were the great Christmas and Thanksgiving celebrations. One of the mixtures of happiness and sadness that goes with being the youngest is seeing one's siblings marry and leave home one by one.

As did my older sisters, I attended Holy Trinity Elementary School taught by the Sisters of Providence. When it was time for high school, you might say that I was following the crowd again, since I had not made a deliberate choice myself. My five older sisters had attended Presentation Academy in Louisville, so I followed them again. I was the only Tighe at Presentation at the time, since my next older sister had just graduated. In high school, I was taught by the Sisters of Charity of Nazareth, Kentucky. Both of the religious communities who taught me had a significant role in influencing my ultimate life choice. While both groups contributed much to my Christian education and faith formation, it is amazing how I can point to two seemingly insignificant "happenings" as real turning points in my calling to religious life.

#1 As an eighth grader I remember that on Saint Valentine's Day some of the boys left the playground during the lunch hour (a forbidden act!) to go downtown to buy candy for their girl friends. When we returned to the classroom after the noon recess, there was much hubbub and I thought to myself, "Sister isn't going to like this!" However, when she appeared at the door she quietly assessed the situation. When she discovered what the excitement was all about she simply said, "Isn't love grand!" It was years later that I realized that Sister Viola Marie, in a most unassuming way, was exemplifying the charism of the Sisters of Providence by showing "love, mercy, and justice" instead of delivering a tirade. Later I realized how that simple event was the seed of my vocation.

#2. Then when I went on to high school the next year, my freshman homeroom teacher provided the second "happening". One evening in the middle of a mission bazaar, as people were going and coming in all directions, Sister Louise de Marillac said to me,

"Did anyone ever tell you that you might have a vocation to become a religious sister?"

My simple answer was, "No, Sister." That was the end of the conversation. She did not say, "Well, I think you do." or "Let's talk about it later." The next morning I awakened thinking about that question. I did not say anything about it at home, but I went down to see one of the priests in our parish, Father Tom Carey. When I told him what had happened, he told me that we would talk about it more, but he suggested that I not speak of it to my parents until we had had more time to examine the idea. Then one day, some months later, he asked me to think about what community I would like to join if I were to follow such a call. Without hesitation I said, "Sisters of Providence." I loved the Sisters of Charity, and especially my homeroom teacher, but something in the Sisters of Providence matched something in me. When I said that I wanted to be a Sister of Providence, Father Carey said, "Thanks be to God!" I think his asking me to wait before I spoke with my parents was because he thought I might have been responding too quickly to the question presented to me by the Sister of Charity. When I wanted to go to another community, I think that made him feel that it was a genuine call. Both Father Carey and I thought highly of the Sisters of Charity, so his "Thanks be to God" was not a rejection of them, but an affirmation of what seemed to be a genuine call to me.

I told my parents on May 5, 1939, their thirtieth wedding anniversary. I was nearing the end of my freshman year. My father's wise words were, "You are too young". Since I was asking only to finish my high school education at Saint Mary-of-the-Woods, he said later, "If you still want to go after your sophomore year you can." I don't think he was absolutely delighted with the idea, but he didn't want to thwart the first movement of what might have been God's invitation. My mother was so utterly surprised that all she could say was, "But you like to play basketball!" With a little time she recovered from the shock. In the

1940 — With my parents on the way to the New York World's Fair

summer of 1940, my parents planned a wonderful trip for the three of us. We went to Washington, D.C. and then on to New York for the World's Fair and to see the play, "Life with Father," on Broadway. We went to Niagara Falls and then on an overnight boat trip across Lake Erie. I am sure that my parents thought I would never again have the chance to see anything beyond the hallowed walls of the convent. My actual date for entering the novitiate was almost two years away. As this story unfolds you will see that my various ministries over the past sixty plus years have taken me far beyond that 1940 vacation.

At the beginning of my junior year I transferred to Providence Juniorate, a high school at Saint Mary-of-the-Woods for young women who thought they might be called to religious life. It was a boarding school from which we returned home for an extended Christmas vacation and for three months in the summer. Today such a school is a rarity, if any at all exist. Most women today enter religious life after college, graduate studies, or even after a number of years in a professional career. I arrived on those hallowed grounds on September 15, 1940. On October 22, 1940, I was there to celebrate the centennial of the foundation of the community by Saint Mother Theodore Guerin.

She had come here from Ruillé-sur-Loir, France, with five other sisters to make the American foundation of the Sisters of Providence who had been founded in France in 1806. The centennial was a wonderful occasion and an unforeseen prelude to another great October day. On October 15, 2006, Mother Theodore would be proclaimed a Saint by Pope Benedict XVI. Little did I realize in 1940, that I would be given an important role to play in that process.

1942 — With my five sisters on the evening before entering the novitiate (front right)

The high school I was entering in my junior year had fewer than one hundred students at that time. We were a close knit group and had many enjoyable times together. Our classes were small, well taught, and rather intense. Because we did not have an abundance of outside activities, the academic schedule allowed us to complete all of our high school credits in three and one-half years. In the summer of 1941, we had a three months' vacation at home. In that same year our Christmas vacation began on December 14, 1941, and ended on January 7, 1942.

So many aspects of my life have helped me to see God's Providential love and action. Going to Saint Mary-of-the Woods for this year and a half with two Christmas vacations and a summer vacation at home allowed me to break away gradually from my dearly loved parents and family. At the end of my Christmas vacation in 1942, I was making the final breakaway. On the night of January 6, all of my older sisters decided that we ought to dress up in formals for the occasion. My parents were there, of course, so we had our last evening together as a family and we did it in grand style. Pictures were taken, and in spite of a certain sadness, it was an enjoyable evening. That night, after I had gone to bed, I remember my mother coming in to tell me good night. She said, "Remember, if you feel that you cannot stay at Saint Mary's you can always come home." There was no pressure, but a beautiful invitation and a good night kiss.

On January 7, 1942, I entered Providence Novitiate. That was exactly one month to the day since the bombing of Pearl Harbor on December 7, 1941. World War II had begun. Entering a novitiate at that time was very much like entering a cloistered life. We spent almost the first three years of World War II with minimal access to world events. We did not read newspapers or listen to the radio. Television was in its infancy. (I remember having seen television for the first time at the New York World's Fair in the summer of 1940.) Much of what we knew of the war came through correspondence with families. We sometimes learned that brothers of novices or postulants had been sent overseas or had been killed. The customs of different religious communities varied at that time in regard to what "leaving one's home" really meant. For our congregation at that time, it meant that I would not return to my home unless my mother or father were in danger of death or had died. As it happened, my mother died rather suddenly seven years after my entrance into the novitiate. My first time back home was in 1949, when I went to New Albany to attend her funeral. These rigid regulations changed some years later.

Upon entering the novitiate, we spent six months as postulants. The word "postulant" means "one who asks." We were asking to be formally received into the novitiate. After the first three months we were asked to choose a name by which we would be known in religious life. The custom was one way of indicating that we were changing our way of life, something comparable to a woman who takes the name of her husband. We could submit three choices and one would be chosen for us. I submitted Kevin Marie, Marie Kevin, and Brigid Ann. My director said, "I think Kevin Marie sounds as if you really want Marie Kevin and can't have it." I knew from that remark that Marie Kevin would be my religious name. On Easter Sunday, April 5, 1942, each postulant knelt before the Superior General and had a small black cap placed on her head. She heard the words, "In religious life you will be known as ...." Many years later we were given the option of returning to our baptismal names. I followed the advice of family members and kept the name Marie Kevin. The family thought the change would cause too much confusion. The fact is that they had always called me Anna, so there was no confusion for them!

As postulants we attended regular classes at Saint Mary-of-the-Woods College. The half-year as postulants was a period of mutual testing. The community was evaluating me and I was evaluating the community. The purpose of this testing period was to see if there was a genuinely mutual "fit." The whole period of postulancy and novitiate was something like the period of engagement prior to marriage. At the end of our postulancy we received the religious habit. Two more years followed before we made profession of temporary vows for one year. The first year was called "Canonical Year" since it was required by the Canon Law of the Church. During that year as canonical novices our studies were limited to those of Scripture, Church History, our SP Constitutions and religious life in general. There were extended times of prayer, as well as group and individual conferences with our Director of Novices. The second year of novitiate at that time was called the "Scholastic Year" and we returned to college classes, while continuing to be instructed in the ways of religious life. About mid-way through the second semester of scholastic year, the General Superior and her Council, having heard the

Novice Director, made the decision about admission to first vows. In my group or "band" as we called it, all of us were approved. We were then known as "Profession Novices." I consider it a special grace from God that my time in the novitiate was one of much peace and happiness. I had had a wonderful family life at home. I continued to love and cherish my parents and sisters, but I did not find myself pining away for them. We often hear the term, "grace of vocation." I am sure that that was what enabled me to move ahead with a call that had come quite unexpectedly and simply during my early teen-age years. On August 15, 1944, we professed temporary vows for one year. Our vow formula follows.

> "Almighty and eternal God, wishing to consecrate myself to your service under the special protection of Jesus, Mary, and Joseph, of my full and deliberate will, I, Sister Marie Kevin Tighe, take for one year the vows of poverty, chastity, and obedience, according to the Constitutions approved by the Holy See for this Congregation of the Sisters of Providence. Grant me, O my God, the grace to be faithful to them until death. In the name of the Father and of the Son and of the Holy Spirit. Amen."
> (Then placing one's right hand on the Bible each one said:
> "So help me God and these Holy Gospels" and then kissed the opened Bible.)

For two consecutive years vows were taken for one year. At the end of the second year, three-year vows were pronounced. At the expiration of three-year vows, perpetual vows completed the commitment. Before final vows, we spent six months back at the Motherhouse in a time of preparation called "Second Novitiate." During that time we made a thirty-day silent retreat directed by a very holy woman, Sister Gertrude Clare Owens. Then came the day of our perpetual vows, August 15, 1949.

At the end of the ceremony, it was the custom in those days for the Bishop who had presided at the vow ceremony, to read the "Obedience List" assigning each Sister of Providence to her place of mission. All of the visitors, who had attended the ceremonies, would leave the church at this point and be replaced by more than one thousand sisters who were present each summer. We filled the main body of the church as well as the crypt where sound from the upper church was projected. When the Bishop re-entered the sanctuary, the Secretary General stepped up and handed him a book with all of our names and assignments. We knelt until we heard our names called and then we were seated. The list began with Indiana and then moved around the country. The farther away we were being sent the longer we knelt! The only ones who had been given advance notice were new local superiors and those going to the foreign missions. It is our custom that one is not sent to a foreign mission unless she volunteers. We had all left our previous assignments in June, packed as if we were never to return. That was necessary in the event that our services were needed elsewhere or someone else needed a transfer for one reason or another. This event kept clear in our minds and hearts the meaning of the vow of obedience. When we left the church after having heard the list read, we found posted in the hallways the information about our departures the next day. This was the accepted way of doing things at that time and we all seemed to have lived through it, even though it provided some bit of anxiety. In spite of that, it did give one a clear sense of having been sent to do the work of the Church and to fulfill the mandate of Jesus to "Go and teach all nations..." At that time our congregation was chiefly engaged in formal education at all levels. Since then we have diversified our ministries and we now have sisters engaged in a variety of the corporal and spiritual works of mercy. Sometimes this was a clear congregation decision to move into another field and sometimes it was the result of the changing composition and talents of the new membership.

Let us look now at religious life and my place in it between 1944 and 1962, that is, from my first teaching assignment until the opening of the Second Vatican Council. This will be a brief sketch, but I would like for you to know what life was like for us before the Council. Our congregation is classified as an active apostolic community, which distinguishes us from cloistered contemplative groups. However, when the active apostolic communities began to emerge, many of the characteristics of the cloistered groups carried over and were added to the lives of the apostolic communities. For example, my first assignment from 1944 until 1949 was as seventh grade teacher at Saint Sylvester School near Humboldt Park on the northwest side of Chicago. There were seventeen Sisters of Providence in our local community. We wore a religious habit similar to those worn for many years - sometimes for centuries - by enclosed orders of contemplative nuns. Our daily schedule, or horarium, was comparable to the cloistered groups, also. Our horarium looked something like this:

4:50	Rising Bell
5:20	Morning Prayer followed by Meditation and the Little Office of the Blessed Virgin
6:30	Communion Service in our chapel
7:00	Breakfast
7:30	Daily house employment
8:00	Mass with all of the children in the parish church
8:45	Classes
3:00	Dismissal
4:30	Community Prayers and Spiritual Reading
6:00	Supper with Spiritual Reading (unless it was a special feast)
6:30	Study Hour
7:30	Recreation
8:30	Night Prayer in Common
9:30	Lights Out

This schedule lasted for me until the mid-60's when some of the modifications following the Second Vatican Council began to emerge. It was recognized that the active religious were spending almost as much time in the chapel as the contemplatives and that, while being fully employed in the external apostolate as well. Schedules began to change to make them more compatible with the active apostolic life.

I can truly say that my pre-Vatican Council II years in this community, 1944-1962 were peaceful and enriching. I was privileged to have lived with many Sisters of Providence who were both a support and an inspiration to me. Since we lived something of an "enclosed" life we came to know each other well. We created our own entertainment as we did not frequent movies, and television did not make its entry into convent life for us until the early 50's. We were quite limited in its usage at the beginning. For most of my pre-Vatican II years in community I was a junior high school teacher. For six of those years I was principal of an elementary school. During that time I hired the first lay teacher for Saint Anne School in New Castle, Indiana. She was an excellent teacher and an exemplary Catholic woman. At that time we were on the very eve of the opening of the Second Vatican Council. It was 1960! It was that Council which so beautifully enhanced the role of the laity in the life of the Church. I continue to be amazed at the events in my life prior to that Council. They opened my mind and heart to the vision of the Church that would be proclaimed to us in the forthcoming call to renewal in the Church, and in religious life, as a sub-unit of the Church. In 1961, I left New Castle after receiving an assignment to be one of three Sisters of Providence to open a new school in Indianapolis. That was another change in my life, but it was a minor change given the fact that the Second Vatican Council would open the next year. That Council would call for a renewed self-understanding of the Church in all of its dimensions. This memoir is an attempt to capture in words and symbols some personal and life-changing experiences.

1962-1965 The Second Vatican Council: An Overview

The Second Vatican Council met intermittently in four separate sessions between October 11, 1962, and December 7, 1965. During that time, while there was widespread interest in what was happening at the Council, it took some time for the full impact to touch the Church at large. The teachings of Vatican II were clearly calling us to realize our shared common mission of being the living presence of Jesus in the world of our time. This was not just the mission of the hierarchy and the clergy, or of the religious orders or congregations. We were called to be One People, the People of God. Clergy, religious, and laity were to be closely interrelated and mutually responsible for making God's presence and action felt in our world.

During the time of the Council itself, I was still teaching at the junior high school level. I had my eighth grade class divided into the Commissions of the Council. Each group was assigned to watch the local and diocesan papers as well as television news for anything on the topics coming from their Commissions. One day I invited the pastor to come into the classroom to hear reports from the Commissions. He declined saying, "Nothing good will come from this Council. The Holy Spirit is backed up against the wall." This pastor has long since departed for the heavenly realms, but during his time on earth his position on the Council remained unchanged. I mention this story because we still have persons of this mindset today. Could it be that some of us have backed ourselves up against the wall in an effort to avoid taking on the real challenges presented to the growing and changing Church of our time?

To set the tone for this book, it may be helpful to examine briefly the major thrust of the teachings of the Second Vatican Council. Two of the four core documents are testimonies on the nature and mission of the Church and both of them have been given the distinction of being named "Constitutions" while most of the other documents are called "Decrees," or "Declarations." In this section of the prologue you will see a graph of concentric circles. This graph shows these two documents on the Church at the center along with the Constitution on Divine Revelation and the Constitution on the Sacred Liturgy. In some way, all of the other documents flow from these. They are at the very heart of the Second Vatican Council and state clearly the identity and purpose of the Church. These documents call each of us, and all of us in our basic Church communities, to accept responsibility for more than our own personal spiritual renewal and well-being. We are called as the People of God to make choices together and to support one another in the choices that will contribute to the spiritual and material well-being of all humanity.

The Second Vatican Council was an event that certainly gave us a renewed sense of Church and of our roles as individuals and as groups in making the presence of God a reality for others. This is expressed well by the late Joseph Cardinal Bernardin in his introduction to the book, Vatican II Revisited By Those Who Were There.[4] Even though these words were written over twenty years ago, the Cardinal named four major items for the future agenda of the Church, which still await our consideration and action as the People of God. He says in summary:

1. "We now recognize that we are a universal Church. How do we accomplish unity in the Church while adapting legitimately to a great diversity of cultures? The Church must seek to reconcile the differences and to bridge the chasms between the Northern and Southern hemispheres, between the rich and the poor of the world.

2. In its documents the Council repeated the traditional doctrine about the hierarchical nature of the Church, but it also insisted that the Church is the entire People of God. We need to work out more clearly how these two truths are inter-related - not just on the theoretical level.

3. Related to, but distinct from the question mentioned above, is the question of the role of women in society and in the Church. Because of the deep feelings surrounding this current and future item, the Church also needs to listen prayerfully and act decisively.

4. A final item on the Church's future agenda is social justice. Such a conversation will make us more attentive to the social and economic needs of all humankind. It will force us to examine how we relate to each other within the Church, and it will

demand that our ecclesial life be an apt model of a just and caring community."

As we examine the core of these four "future agenda items" offered two decades back, we see some very current issues to be addressed by us as Church:

- universality – globalization
- hierarchy- People of God
- the role of women
- social justice

To bring this closer to our time, in the Presidential Address at the Leadership Conference of Women Religious held on August 4, 2007, Mary Dacey, SSJ named "global spirituality, dialogue, and the poor" as the key issues to be addressed by that group and the Church at large. She stated that they are "inextricably linked to one another." So when you look at Cardinal Bernardin's four items and Sister Mary Dacey's three, I believe you read a common message.

These agenda items seem to fit what would be needed for a genuine "corporate renewal" in the Church as a whole – as the Body of Christ. This kind of "corporate renewal" is needed in every sub-unit of the Church, beginning with the family, the domestic Church. Then we move to the cluster of families and individuals known as parishes; clusters of parishes known as deaneries; clusters of deaneries known as dioceses/archdioceses. Within dioceses/archdioceses we have presbyterates, pastoral staffs, school faculties, hospital and nursing home staffs, pastoral councils at various levels, religious communities, and many other corporate entities or church units. The ability of each of these groups to prayerfully reflect and dialogue toward decisions, which will authenticate them as Church, as the Mystical Body of Christ, will result in genuine renewal. What Cardinal Bernardin was pointing out to us in his proposed agenda some years after the closing of the Council, is that much needs to be done if the work of the Council is to be implemented and true renewal is to be realized.

"Themes of the Second Vatican Council" [5]

"One has only to glance at the themes of the Council and to try to arrange them in meaningful order to realize the magnitude of the task undertaken. They are:

I. The fundamental self-understanding of the Church in the Dogmatic Constitution on the Church

II. The inner life of the Church:

   A. Her ministry of sanctification notably expressed in the Constitution on the Sacred Liturgy

   B. Her pastoral ministry in the Decree on the Pastoral Office of Bishops in the Church, and the Decree on the Oriental Catholic Churches

   C. Her teaching ministry in the Dogmatic Constitution on Divine Revelation and the Declaration on Christian Education

   D. Her states of life:
     1. Decree on the Ministry and Life of Priests
     2. Decree on the Training of Priests
     3. Decree on the Apostolate of the Laity
     4. Decree on the Adaptation and Renewal of Religious Life

III. The mission of the Church to those outside:

   Decree on Ecumenism
   Decree on Oriental Churches
   Declaration on Non-Christian Religions Including the Jews
   Decree on the Missionary Activity of the Church
   Pastoral Constitution on the Church in the Modern World
   Declaration on Religious Freedom
   Decree on the Instruments of Social Communication"

Marie Kevin Tighe, S.P.

This set of concentric circles is one effort to present at a glance, the scope of the sixteen documents from Vatican Council II. At the core are the Constitutions. The next two rings contain the Decrees, and the three Declarations are in the outer ring. One would be hard pressed to put these documents in the exact order of importance. Suffice it to say, that together these sacred documents call us to a renewed sense of being the Church, the People of God. They call us to personal holiness and to a corporate spirituality. As Church, we are the Mystical Body of Christ. The Council reminds us that we are "to render God present and, as it were visible in the world."

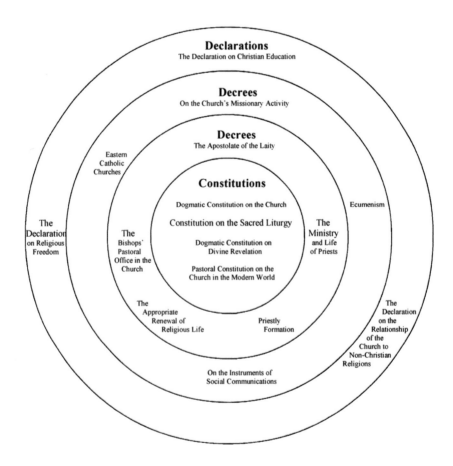

1965-1972 · Years Immediately Following the Council

From 1965 until 1968, I had my first assignment as principal of a co-educational high school. I had completed a graduate degree in secondary school administration. In the state of Indiana that required a double master's degree, that is, more than sixty graduate hours in education and administration. The newness of this assignment somehow interrupted my original intense interest in the teachings of the Council, but I still tried to read and keep abreast of this new age in the Church. In 1968, as I made preparations for the graduation ceremony at Washington Catholic High School, in Washington, Indiana, little did I realize that, in a way, I was preparing for my own "graduation." From this time on, my path would lead me out of secondary education into ministries directly or indirectly related to the teachings of the Second Vatican Council.

From the beginning of the Council, I had had the blessing of feeling that God was calling us to a deeper responsibility as Church. It seemed that much good would come from this insightful response of Pope John XXIII to the action of the Spirit during his pontificate. This gift of openness would serve me well as the next few years of my life would unfold.

In 1967, I celebrated my silver jubilee as a Sister of Providence. In 1968, I was appointed to the Saint Gabriel (Indiana) Regional Council. Up until that time, the Sisters of Providence had a very centralized governance structure, but because we were assigned from coast to coast and in great numbers, Rome

1970 — Newly elected Saint Gabriel Provincial Council (left to right) Sister Mary Maxine Teipen, Provencial, with Sisters Bernice Kuper and Marie Kevin Tighe

suggested that we form provinces. This decentralization was a great step forward in enabling us to exercise greater shared responsibility for our life and mission in the Church. Regions were step one in the process of forming provinces. In this beginning stage, appointments to the regional councils were made by the General Superior. About a year after this step was taken, we were formally established as provinces. In 1970 we held the first provincial elections and I was elected for a four-year term, which was cut short by one of many providential events to be described later. But first, I must share a bit about my four years on the regional/provincial council. During that period of time, there were six-hundred seventeen sisters in our Saint Gabriel Province. Sisters were stationed in approximately seventy locations. One of my responsibilities was overseeing the life and work of our sisters in the eleven Catholic high schools where we had sisters on the faculties. Not all of these were community-owned schools. As Director of Apostolic Works, I also visited sisters engaged in a variety of ministries. We were then in the beginning of the post-conciliar change period. Sisters were encouraged to engage in discernment with the provincial council concerning the best use of their talents and abilities. Some found this very life-giving; others struggled with the concept. It was a time of great freedom of spirit for some, and a time of great confusion and some resistance for others. Then Rome announced that all religious communities were to call a Special General Chapter to deal with the changes called for by the Vatican Council. Our last regular Chapter had been held in 1966. This Special Chapter took place in 1969. One of the things the Council had called us to do was to bring our way of life into conformity with the changed conditions of the times. As stated earlier, many active apostolic communities had over the years adopted lifestyles and religious garb that imitated those of the cloistered communities. There were some elements of "enclosure" when I first entered the congregation. By the 1960's, the pace of public life, and lay involvement in the Church had changed so radically, that it was not helpful to set active religious communities above the dedicated laypersons engaged in the ministries of the church. Because the greater part of our day was spent in the public sector, where we were often in contact with laity who worked side by side with us, our religious garb could give a false message. None of this is to say that the religious state is not a valuable, viable, and honored way of living the Christian life. It is just to say that the way we present ourselves can seem to set us "above" the laity. So in many apostolic communities the formal religious garb was made optional. Not everyone within these communities approved of this decision and certainly not everyone outside these communities understood the rationale. It was thought by some that we were denying our commitments, which certainly was not the case.

As I said, many of the changes were made in our congregation at the time of the Special General Chapter of 1969. I spent the years 1968-1972, moving around our province and talking with more than six hundred sisters. There were varying degrees of understanding regarding many of the changes even among the sisters themselves. For some, the changes were very painful. For others, they made perfectly good sense. The changes involved more than clothing, but that was the most obvious one. There were other more subtle theological differences. This was true, also, beyond the convent walls. We were in a period of transformation and people were in varying degrees of readiness for what this required of us.

Something more was needed to help us move beyond our individual positions on matters of the moment. We needed to come together in a new way, one that would be a process of mutual re-education and mutual conversion. Simply taking positions would not be helpful, because taking positions that cannot be examined, expanded, or even changed means that someone believes that her truth is the whole truth or the only truth.

In God's loving Providence that "something more" that was needed was offered to us. We now approach the major topics of this memoir and how the Arch, Steeples, and Dome were powerful religious symbols on my journey of faith, my life.

Part I.
The Arch
1972 – 1980

On the Banks of the Mississippi River, in the city of Saint Louis, Missouri, stands a beautifully designed Arch signifying the Gateway to the West. In 1972, not many years after the closing of the Second Vatican Council, that Arch became a very significant religious symbol for me. It was in Saint Louis, together with five other Sisters of Providence, that I was introduced to the principles of corporate renewal, which for the next twenty years would be the foundation for my ministry. The Arch symbolized the Church as an open passageway to heaven for all peoples. Its graceful openness was a reminder of the call of Pope John XXIII, to open the windows of the Church. This called for a renewed understanding of the Church as the People of God, and for new modes of participation at all levels of Church life. This could not happen simply by reading the Council documents. It required a conversion of personal and group interaction that could result in genuine dialogue and collaborative decision-making.

What I learned and experienced on the other side of the Arch has profoundly impacted my life as a woman religious, a woman of the Church.

Part I. The Arch (1972-1980)
A. A New Frontier

It seems Providential to me that it was in the city of Saint Louis, in the shadow of one of the most unusual landmarks in our country, that a new frontier was opened for my community and for me. Now the Arch was not only the symbol of the Gateway to the West of our country, but a symbol of the windows of the Church opened to the world.

It was in this place that I had the opportunity with five other sisters from my community of the Sisters of Providence of Saint Mary-of-the-Woods, Indiana, to learn new ways of facilitating the implementation of some of the major changes called for by Vatican II. What was learned was useful not only in my own community, but as this story unfolds you will see how this experience touched many aspects of the larger Church. Because of this opportunity, I think of Saint Louis as the "Promised Land" for renewal. This is because two "Wise Men" from the Gateway to the West had a vision, and a plan to realize it. Their story will follow the account of the mysterious way in which I arrived at the Arch.

The document on the Renewal of Religious Life stated: "The up-to-date renewal of the religious life comprises both a constant return to the sources of the whole of the Christian life and to the primitive inspiration of the institutes and their adaptation to the changed conditions of our times."[6] It further stated, "Effective renewal and right adaptation cannot be achieved save with the cooperation of all the members of an institute."[7] This last sentence was brief but radical in its meaning for religious communities. It was calling us to a new kind of shared responsibility for the life and mission of our congregations. In another radical shift in the concept of authority, the document further stated, "Superiors, in matters which concern the destiny of the entire institute. should find appropriate means of consulting their subjects, and should listen to them."[8] These statements were in no way intended to weaken or to eradicate the authority of office held by those duly elected. They simply called for the recognition of the authority of personhood in each member, and the authority of the community as a corporate whole. These three dimensions of authority were called to work together to discern prayerfully the kinds of changes needed for this new era in church and world history.

In 1972, our General Superior and her Council heard of an Institute in Saint Louis that seemed to be just what was needed to enable this process to take place. Because of the size and geographical spread of our congregation at that time, it was thought that at least six sisters would need to be relieved from all other duties for a minimum of two years. This group would go through an intense period of training and then assist the congregation in developing the skills needed for collaborative decision-making. When the Council had made the decision to engage this process, it remained to be determined how the six sisters would be chosen. From the outset, shared responsibility was built into this first decision. Each local community in the congregation was asked to nominate three sisters for the team. When the nominations came in, each nominee was called. Some had to decline because of being involved in a phase or aspect of their ministry that would be hard to hand over at the time. The training staff interviewed and tested the willing nominees. After going through many nominees and trying to combine complementary gifts, the team was finally chosen. It was the spring of 1972. I ended up being one of the six members of the team, although not one of the original six. How did this happen? Permit me to backtrack a bit to share this story.

As mentioned earlier, I was a member of the Saint Gabriel (Indiana) Provincial Council from 1968-1972. My term of office would not have been completed until 1974. When nominees were being considered for the renewal team, I was not eligible. The trainers had determined that no one on a Provincial or General Council should be on the team. The team was supposed to represent the grassroots thinking. One of my responsibilities as a Council member was to visit our sister-students at Saint Louis University to see how their studies were progressing and to discuss with them their future ministries. When I arrived in Saint Louis that spring, I had not yet heard that the team had been finalized, but I discovered while there, that the team had been named. I was able to learn a little more about the nature and scope of the training and I became more and more enthusiastic about the possibilities I saw in this for the renewal in our community – and even beyond! Later I learned that my enthusiasm had been communicated to the trainers.

I returned to Saint Mary-of-the-Woods for our General Chapter of 1972. One day, near the closing of this community meeting, I was sitting in the chapel early in the morning. The thought came to me, "I am going back to our Provincial House and in and out of the back door with my suitcase, and in and out of all of those houses. I am not sure that what we are doing now is helping us in this time of so much change." Suddenly, (without any voice being heard!) the thought came to me, "Stop thinking about yourself." It startled me somewhat. I left the chapel. When I reached the vestibule, our General Secretary, Sister Ann Kathleen Brawley, was standing there. She said, "We received a call from Saint Louis. They heard of your enthusiasm for the team effort and they want to know if you will resign from the Provincial Council and replace Sister Alexa Suelzer who was chosen for the renewal team, but who has just been elected to the General Council." That was my second surprise of the morning! I said, "Let me talk to Mother Mary Pius." When I found her, she said, "You know, this morning when you were in the chapel, I was in the gallery. I was praying that you would be willing to do this." I have often described this as one of the most identifiable "God-moments" of my life. In a flash, the whole course of my life changed, not just for a few days or weeks, but for the rest of my years!

Having been elected at the 1970 Provincial Chapter for a four-year term, as I said, I was not supposed to have gone out of office until 1974. It was then July of 1972, so another sister was appointed to replace me on the Council. I was a delegate to our General Chapter of 1972, when I learned that I was going to be a replacement on the Renewal Team. When the Chapter was over, I drove to Saint Louis. The training had already begun. I think the others had arrived about a week ahead of me. I soon caught on that this

1972 — The members of the Cor Unum Renewal Team (on left)

was going to be an intense experience. The rest of the team helped me to play "catch-up." The actual content and process of our training will be found in the segment of this book entitled, "Individual and Corporate Renewal."

The training period took place under the direction of a staff of fourteen highly professional persons. Concerned with developing internal resources for renewal, the institute had this basic premise: "Religious presence is most effective when there is a deep understanding among the members of what it means to be 'a corporate people of mission.' Renewal has always aimed at recapturing in the community of today the spirit with which it began." So, for us as Sisters of Providence of Saint Mary-of-the-Woods, corporate discernment toward a genuine renewal is a process of searching and sharing together around the vision and mission of Saint Mother Theodore Guerin. It is to rediscover, again and again, in the light of the Gospel and of our living tradition, how we are to express our original spirit in a manner suited to the changing circumstances of our world. Whatever "gaps" may be disclosed through our common searching and sharing would provide the arena for corporate decision-making and renewal.

In August of 1972 the team returned to the Motherhouse, well-instructed and well-armed for the work that was ahead of us. The task was a monumental one: to engage more than twelve hundred sisters in discovering which issues needed further corporate study and then probing those issues in terms of: the person of Christ, the spirit of the founding person, and the historical mission of the Church. The outcome of all of this was aimed at:

- a deepening of the commitment of the sisters to one another
- a developing of the capacity for corporate faith-sharing and decision-making
- a clarifying of the spirit, vision, and mission to which this community aspires
- a statement of commitment on specific community issues

The team chose the name "Cor Unum," a name that captured the purpose of its mission within the Congregation. What a powerful effect outward the Congregation would have if it could always be perceived as acting with one heart!

The Renewal Team was commissioned to serve for a minimum of two years with six members. It was suggested by the trainers that the team would gradually phase itself out, after having built the renewal process into the existing structures. In the first two years, there were six full-time members; in the third year there were four full-time members; in the first six months of the fourth year there were three full-time members and in the last six months of the fourth year there were two full-time members. As of July, 1976, the process of corporate renewal was to be considered self-sustaining through the existing structures of the Congregation: Chapters, Councils, Communities and Committees. Corporate Reflection Centers would be coordinated through the existing provincial structures and directed by sisters within each province. Later as we moved from Provinces to Local Government Units, what had been learned and practiced during these early days of renewal continued to bear fruit.

(In the fall of 2008, I conducted a survey of our Congregation just to assess, in an informal way, how our sisters had experienced these years of renewal. The returns exceeded by 17% the required number needed for an accurate reading of a group. This information was gleaned from www.researchinfo.com. In general, the sisters felt that we had done slightly better on adaptation than on renewal. However, one of the strongest responses in the positive category was that there was a deepened appreciation and understanding of the charism of our founding person, Saint Mother Theodore Guerin. This is crucial to the ongoing life of any religious group. Second to this, was the strong positive response saying that we had learned the importance of collaboration and shared responsibility in our community gatherings. There were other responses that indicated a need for further dialogue regarding our identity and the need to examine our power of attracting new members to this Congregation in this radically different period of time.)

By the summer of 1976 most of the original Cor Unum Team had assumed new responsibilities. By this time, The Institute for the Development of Internal Resources for Renewal ($I^2 R^2$) had changed its name to The Center for Planned Change. I received a call asking if I would consider joining the staff of CPC. After having this approved by my superior, I moved again "beyond the Arch." This opportunity allowed me to take what I had learned to a broader area of the Church. Once more Saint Louis became a "New Frontier."

The four years, 1976-1980, were full and rich beyond measure, as I had the opportunity to work not only with thirty other religious communities, but with various formal church structures: archdioceses, dioceses, and presbyterates.* As I moved into these other arenas, it was truly amazing to see how thorough our training in corporate renewal had been. I realized how solidly and soundly the basic principles of corporate theological reflection and those of the psychology of organizations, if carefully understood and wedded to the task, could contribute to a renewal of life in the Church.

Just as the Second Vatican Council opened the windows of the Church to those who had read the documents aright, so the Arch at Saint Louis opened my eyes to the broader Church and strengthened my already deep love of the Church. I will try to share here briefly an experience, which convinced me of the validity of the concept of corporate renewal.

*See listing at the end of this section.

For the calendar year 1978, I was assigned as assistant project director to a large archdiocese that had shown some interest in engaging the process. The Archbishop wanted to be sure that he had the commitment of his priests and people before committing to a "Year of Learning for Pastoral Planning in a Collaborative Style." In order to gain this commitment, one hundred-fifty persons were brought together for a week of reflection and discernment. Everyone arrived at a secluded retreat house on a Sunday afternoon and amazingly, no one left until the following Friday afternoon. The first step was to develop a set of common criteria for examining the proposal. The first two days were spent in "Ecclesial Groups" made up of bishops, priests, superiors of men's orders or congregations, superiors of women's communities, and lay persons from various regions of the archdiocese. After two days in "Ecclesial Groups," they spent two days in "Role Groups." So, for example, when the priests' "Role Group" met each priest was coming from a different "Ecclesial Group," thereby having had his own personal vision broadened and enlightened. At the conclusion, the Archbishop was asked to sit on a swivel chair in the middle of the room, since as head of a large archdiocese he couldn't look in one direction too long! In a single final session, the role groups reported and there was unanimous agreement to engage the process with some minor variations on the proposal. Every other month for a year a comparable session was held in different parts of the archdiocese. The Archbishop was present for these meetings and heard the various pastoral planning needs of the people. A Planning Commission was formed and met monthly with the Archbishop and other officials. This is only a glimpse of the whole process. It was, for me and for others, a true experience of the Church as the People of God working collaboratively to shape the future of a local church.

When we completed the "Year of Learning," we had a celebratory dinner with the Archbishop, the consultants, our staff, and some graduate students who had served as adjunct staff. I remember well the closing words of the Archbishop at that dinner. He said, "Someone has said that parting is sweet sorrow. What makes it sweet is that we all have hearts big enough to take each other with us." That reminded me of our SP Renewal Team's name, "Cor Unum." The realization of that title is one of the goals and purposes of the Church, from the "domestic Church" of the family to the Universal Church throughout the world… one Body, One Heart.

Marie Kevin Tighe, S.P.

My On-Site Assignments with Religious Communities of Women and Men and with Diocesan and Archdiocesan Structures - 1980 – 1992

Women:	Archdioceses, Dioceses, Presbyterates
Burlingame, CA – Sisters of Mercy	
Rapid City, SD – Benedictine Sisters	
San Antonio, TX – Sisters of the Incarnate Word	
Saint Louis, MO – Sisters of the Incarnate Word	Indianapolis (Eight years)
Mequon, WI – School Sisters of Notre Dame	
Portland, ME – Sisters of Mercy *	
Pittsfield, MA – Sister of the Holy Cross	Boston
Richfield, CN – Congregation of Notre Dame	(One year)
Dayton, OH – Congregation of the Precious Blood	
Nazareth, KY – Sister of Charity of Nazareth *	Springfield, IL
Buffalo, NY – Sisters of Mercy	
Boston, MA – Sisters of Saint Joseph *	Lafayette, IN
Lexington, MA – Grey Nuns	
Bethesda, MD – Sisters of Saint Francis	Belleville, IL:
Oldenburg, IN – Sisters of Saint Francis	
Rome, Italy – Religious of the Sacred Heart of Mary *	
London. England – Religious of the Sacred Heart of Mary	
Pennmaenmawr, Wales – Religious of the Sacred Heart of Mary	National Conference for Pastoral Planning and Council Development
Melbourne, KY – Congregation of Diving Providence	
Ruma, IL – Adorers of the Precious Blood	
Chicago, IL – Congregation of the Blessed Virgin Mary	

Owensboro, KY – Passionist Nuns
Mobile, Al – Daughters of Charity
Chicago, IL – Daughters of Charity
Evansville, IN – Daughters of Charity
Monroe, MI – Immaculate Heart of Mary *   Member of the
Columbus, OH – Dominican Sisters   Coordinating
    Committee
Cincinnati, OH – Sister of Charity   Presenter at two
Arlington Heights, IL – Sisters   National
of the Living Word *   Conventions
Saint Mary-of-the-Woods, IN   Los Angeles and
– Sisters of Providence   Sacramento

(* Asterisk denotes facilitation of General Chapter)

Men:
Lafayette, CA – Oblate of Mary Immaculate   Institute of
Houston, TX – Oblates of Mary Immaculate   Religious
Manville, RI – Oblates of Mary Immaculate   Formation
Halifax, Nova Scotia – Oblates   Saint Louis U.
of Mary Immaculate   Presenter for
Montreal, Quebec, Canada –   Ten Years
Congregation of the Holy Cross
Valatie, NY – Congregation of the Holy Cross
Attelboro, MA – La Salette Missionaries

B. Two Prophets

As the Second Vatican Council came to an end, there were two men on the faculty of Saint Louis University whose collaborative wisdom and commitment to the Church, inspired them to make a major contribution to the practical implementation of the vision and call of the Council Documents. One of these men was Father Thomas P. Swift, S.J., a canon lawyer and theologian. The other was Dr. Nick J. Colarelli, a clinical and organizational psychologist. At the conclusion of the Council, and as the documents began to circulate, both of these men were frequently asked to speak to religious communities and to assist them with their efforts to implement what the Church was calling them to do. When they would return to the university after having worked with these groups, Father Swift and Doctor Colarelli would meet to discuss insights and experiences. They soon realized that the kind of renewal needed would not happen by having external speakers addressing and advising. The change required must be the result of internal dialogue and shared decision-making. For groups that had functioned for a century or more in a top-down, authoritarian style of governance, many new attitudes and skills would need to be learned. It required more than an intellectual kind of learning; it required a genuine conversion in personal style of interaction. In religious communities these efforts needed to be rooted in the Gospel, the Constitutions, and the spirit of the founding person. In addition, there must be a clear understanding of the documents of the Council and the shift that was called for in the exercise of authority. That model had moved from the pyramidal to the circular model. The call to mutuality and shared responsibility is really a call to a dual conversion, that of the heart and of the manner of interaction for every member of a community. Two questions emerged as preeminent: 1.) What could be brought to this effort from both the theological and the psychological realms? and 2.) Which groups in the Church seemed most ready to begin this movement toward corporate conversion and renewal?

The two-fold answer to question #1 was:
a.) to initiate a method of corporate theological reflection rooted in the Scriptures, the history, spirit, and tradition of the group involved and the most recent official teaching of the Church from the Second Vatican Council

b.) to help groups understand the elements of organizational life with both the potentials and the threats to that life, which apply to faith communities as well as to other groups with a common purpose.

After "scanning the ecclesial horizon," it seemed that the answer to question # 2 was, that the place to begin would be with congregations of women religious. These "two prophets," that is, teachers "par excellence," had been working with enough groups by this time to have learned that women religious had made valiant, if not always successful, efforts to take up the task of implementing the call of the Church for renewal.

So what followed was the formation of The Institute for the Development of Internal Resources for Renewal, or $I^2 R^2$ for the short title.

When I speak of Father Swift and Doctor Colarelli as prophets, I am convinced that they deserve that title. In their separate fields they were both excellent teachers. While the word prophet does not always mean one who foretells the future, in a sense, these two men foresaw that unless groups took major steps to learn new modes of being together for the life and mission of the Church, the truly wonderful teachings of the Council would remain dead letters. It is at this point that I wish to give a quote from Karl Rahner, S.J. who wrote these words about five years before our "two prophets" made a leap in faith.

> "It will certainly be a long time before the Church which has been given the Second Vatican Council will become the Church of the Second Vatican Council, just as it took a number of generations after the close of the Council of Trent before she became the Church of the Reform of Trent. But this does not alter in the least our own terrible responsibility, which we all who are in the Church have been invited to fulfill: to do what we have said we will do, to become that which we have recognized ourselves to be, to make deeds out of words, to make spirit out of rules, to make true prayer out of liturgical forms, and reality out of ideas. The Council could hardly be more than the beginning of this task, but that is a great deal, and it is more than can be expressed in mere words."[9]

It was a true moment of grace for many religious congregations and for the Church-at-large, when these insightful and faith-filled men recognized how their very diverse professional areas complemented one another. Father Swift's background in theology and Canon Law and Doctor Colarelli's training in both clinical and organizational psychology were vital to the kind of learning needed to implement the collaborative relationships in the Church that were called for by the Council. As these lines are being written other books are appearing to remind us that we have not fully implemented the Council's directives. (These books are mentioned in the Introduction to this book.) What the "two prophets" recognized was, that in order to implement the basic teachings of the Council, new understandings of Church, new behaviors, genuine dialogue and response to the call for shared responsibility, were essential. This needed to be encouraged by the episcopate and clergy and embraced by the laity. That did not happen in broad strokes over the Universal Church. Here and there efforts were made. Then appeared the "Two Prophets."

In the summer of 1971, only six years after the closing of Vatican II, the first teams of women religious were formed and trained to initiate a process of Corporate Renewal in their congregations. In 1972, my religious community sent a team to be trained. As I understand it, this approach to providing congregations with assistance in their renewal efforts was never submitted to the open market by advertising. Personal interviews with General Councils by Father Swift, Doctor Colarelli, or other colleagues, were required to determine the readiness of a group for such a venture. It was essential that an entire council be present for the deliberations and commitment to the formation of a renewal team. Once teams were chosen, a period of intense training began. Teams were asked to come prepared with internal documents such as community histories and Constitutions.

We learned early on, that the basic assumption regarding the concept of corporate renewal is this: If there is to be direction, depth, and form to our shared life and mission, it is important that we discover together some common ground for examining, evaluating and planning our approach to renewal, which is a call to change, conversion, transformation. It was this basic assumption, which made the "wedding" of the theological and organizational aspects of this Institute so effective for the groups that embraced it whole-heartedly. Since a religious community, or for that matter, any segment of the Universal Church, is an organization, it is essential for us to have an understanding of what an organization is and how it functions. We must understand the individual in relationship to the organization, as well as have an awareness of one another as <u>persons</u>, as <u>persons-within-the-group</u>, and as <u>a group</u>. (Each of the underlined words is a different reality.) We must continually search together for that to which we are called in each new moment, always maintaining our historical identity and integrity while employing the means of contemporary discernment and adaptation to the changed conditions of the times in which we live. Renewal does not mean throwing off the past and the foundational truths, which define our identity. Rather, renewal is a deepening of those defining characteristics, but with adaptation that will strengthen our identity and purpose in a new moment of time. The calling forth of a team of persons, internal to each congregation, was for the purpose of engaging the community in a process of corporate reflection on their charism and mission. This aimed at helping the members of the congregation to reflect upon their experience, to generate options for action, and to make choices that embodied the deepest values of the group. Simply put, this is known as the ERCA model – Experience, Reflection, Choice and Action. To attempt to build this into a group's life process was a daunting task. In our Congregation, efforts were valiant on the part of the community and on the part of the team.

    The following will be a description of the training as I experienced it. Our team was composed of six Sisters of Providence ranging in age from sixty-two to twenty-six. Time had to be spent in learning to know and to understand each other. It was important to learn each one's special gifts and strengths for team development. We prayed together and shared life stories. We discussed our community history and the story of our founding sister, who is now Saint Mother Theodore Guerin. The work of all renewal is to be rooted and grounded in one's own personal and community history. We were trained with sisters from eight other congregations of women religious. Interacting with sisters from other traditions, charisms, and histories, helped us to see the uniqueness of each group and to understand our own uniqueness so much better.

    The training period was set up in what might be called a "saturation design." It was a five-week period of days that were rarely less than ten hours in length. The well-trained staff of fourteen persons had been chosen by Father Swift and Doctor Colarelli. They modeled for us what it meant to work as a team with a common purpose. Our days were spent in prayer, liturgy, lectures, and small group development. My personal assessment of this training period is that it was one of my most intense, comprehensive, and life-giving learning experiences. I believe that it was even more. It was a conversion experience.

I intend, by the very title given to this brief segment, to express to these "Two Prophets," the gratitude of the thousands of recipients of their untiring efforts. They helped to make the teachings of the Vatican Council come alive in a way that, I believe, is unique in the long post-conciliar period. Both men gave not only their wisdom and knowledge, but they gave of their very lives. Family life, community life, and professional life, were sacrificed to some extent by both men. How true it is that prophets of any nature are rarely given their proper acclaim! Here I express my eternal gratitude.

A basic description of our training will be found in the next section entitled, "Individual and Corporate Renewal."

C. Individual and Corporate Renewal

In writing of renewal, I am referring to change, growth, conversion, and moving toward integrity and authenticity at the personal and corporate levels. Individual renewal is the lifework of every person. It is our preparation for our eternal life with God for which we were created. Our model for this personal conversion is found in the life of Jesus of Nazareth. He is "the Way and the Truth and the Life." (John 14:6) In the whole of our personal lives we are called again and again to a deeper union with Jesus and to a closer following of Him through the practice of the Christian virtues. Our fidelity to our way of life must be nourished over time by the sacraments, prayer, retreats, spiritual direction and other ways of strengthening and maintaining our union with God. The prayerful and reflective personal choices we make will, with God's help, contribute to our life-long conversion of heart, our personal renewal. This is no small task! There can be no personal renewal or transformation without decisions and actions supported by God's grace. This is true of us as individuals and it is also true of groups, especially groups committed to following Jesus and furthering the life and mission of His Church. We always need to discern whether or not our personal and communal choices are integrating and authenticating or debilitating and destructive in light of our call to be followers of Jesus, to be the Church, the Mystical Body of Christ in the here and now.

While individual renewal is challenging enough for most of us, the call to renewal of the various ecclesial groups to which we belong is even more of a challenge. However, we must always remember that individual and corporate renewal work "hand-in-glove," so to speak. It is very difficult, of not impossible, to have one without the other. This is true of the smallest social and ecclesial group, the family, and moves on through parishes, dioceses, religious communities, and on to the Church Universal. In order to understand the corporate renewal of these groups, we must realize that by force of numbers, these groups have all of the dimensions of organizational life. It is often the case that when this is not adequately understood, individuals are blamed for what seems to be dysfunction or lack of realization of group goals. What needs to be examined to avoid this error is to learn the basics of organizational subsystems. The problem is more likely to be systemic than personal. Let us examine this theory briefly now.

Every social system has five basic interdependent subsystems. A weakness or a breakdown in any one of them affects all of the others. The five subsystems are: 1.) Authority, 2.) Maintenance, 3.) Boundary, 4.) Adaptive, and 5.) Productive. Let us use the example of these subsystems in a religious community, post-Vatican II.

Authority   is the relational power associated with a position, the purpose of which is to coordinate the mission and to maintain communication throughout the congregation (system).

Because the Vatican Council called for shared responsibility, authority in the Church rests on a tripod: a.) Authority of Office, b.) Authority of Personhood, c.) Authority of the Community as a Corporate Person. This shared responsibility in no way diminishes the authority of office. It simply requires that authority is to be exercised in a more collaborative way with all of the members of a community, especially in those matters which affect the whole community

Maintenance   is the function, which enables persons to grow and to develop as productive members. Some examples of events or opportunities, which "maintain" and "enhance" members of a religious community are: prayer, community living, ministry assignments, education, recreation, health care, etc.

Boundary   is the differentiation, which distinguishes one group from another. Boundaries must be permeable enough to take in newness, that is, new ideas, new members, new information, but defined enough to maintain the identity and integrity of the group.

Adaptive   is the ability to adjust to changed cultural and temporal environments and circumstances, while at the same time preserving the nature and purpose of the congregation. Adapting means changing to meet the needs of a changing environment, without necessarily adopting

Productive   This subsystem indicates the accomplishment of the overall purpose of the institute. For religious communities which are apostolic in nature this would include the quality of religious presence, the sanctification of the members, and the apostolic effectiveness of the group in its outward mission or purpose.

all of the values of that environment or abandoning a group's own core values.

All of these subsystems are operative in every dimension of ecclesial life beginning with the domestic Church of the family and extending to parishes, presbyterates, seminaries, and moving on to include all of the various church organizations, which we know today. They are also applicable to the highest offices of the Church such as the Roman Curia, the Pontifical Congregations, and Ecumenical Councils.

Group Climate;

As we continue to engage the topic of corporate renewal, it is essential to address the topic of group climate. It is difficult to think of any one factor more important to group life and effectiveness than that of climate. Climate is the general feeling tone of a group. Climate is created by the quality of relationships that exists between and among the members of a group and the level of understanding and commitment that persons have regarding their common purpose. While working on a project in Boston, I had the distinct honor and pleasure of working briefly with Dr. Freed Bales of Harvard University. At that time he was in the process of writing a book entitled, SYMLOG, an acronym for Systemic Multi-level Observation of Groups.[10] On the next page I will show an interesting graph from his book, which gives one way to understand the dimensions of group climate.

"Systemic Multi-Level Observation of Groups" (SYMLOG)
Dr. Freed H. Bales, Ph.D.

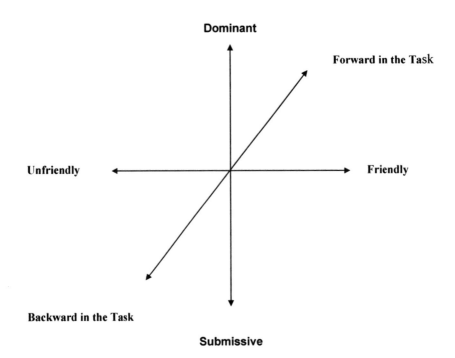

My simple description of this graph follows.

An effective and life-giving group would be found in the upper right-hand quadrant of this graph. The word "dominant" does not mean dominating, but rather, committed and fully participating. The word "task" could refer to a specific task or to the overall mission of a group. Obviously, to be in a group that lives and works in the lower left hand quadrant would be deadening and unproductive. However, if a group wanted to renew itself, it could use an instrument such as this to reflect, choose, and act corporately, thus improving the climate and effecting new life for the membership and its overall mission.

The Individual;
The Individual-in-Community;
The Community as a Corporate Person

The first of these three realities is most easily understood. We experience it in our own persons. As individuals, each of us has a family of origin, a unique life history, a particular way of being-in-the-world. Each of us has a faith life, a set of personal values, an accumulation of knowledge and a worldview. This is to name but a few of our individual characteristics. When we experience ourselves as an individual-in-the-group, it is a new reality. We are enhanced or inhibited by the differences we discern among us. If we are particularly astute and capable of recognizing the richness to be gained by the gifts, talents, insights and perspectives of others, we find this new reality to be a life-giving experience. However, in some ways it will call for a change in the way we reach decisions and express our individuality. If we find that we can move beyond being aware only of being an-individual-in-a-group, and have a genuine experience of the group becoming a community of persons, with a new corporate identity, we have, indeed, reached a creative moment in our existence. We have come to the realization that the community has a life of its own that is different from the life of any one member in it, and more than just the sum of the lives if its members. In the many sub-units of the Church, and in the Church as a whole, this is the realization of what it means to be the Church – the Mystical Body of Christ. It is in the spirit of the Founding Person, namely, Jesus, that we have come together to be and to do what no one of us could be or do alone. This same principle carried to another level of Church, such as a religious order or congregation, helps us to understand the importance of strengthening and maintaining the founding spirit of the one who received from God a specific charism or gift of the Spirit. Maintaining this original spirit is essential to the on-going life of the community. Fidelity to that charism will allow a group not only to survive, but to flourish in a meaningful and effective manner no matter what the times and the world scene present.

Marie Kevin Tighe, S.P.

Recognizing the Community of Faith as a Human Organization

It serves us well, as communities of faith, to recognize that our common history, our common bonds, and our common mission, as well as the number of persons involved, place us in the category of a human organization. These two dimensions of our corporate life – faith community and organization – can be mutually beneficial if we understand the inner workings of both. If we try to live and function only as one or the other, instead of as a blend of both, we create a plethora of problems for ourselves. As communities of faith we are rooted in God and bonded to one another in faith. Our coming together in prayer and worship and in the ordinary interactions of daily living, are meant to support our faith life and our Christian mission and ministries. At the same time, we must be aware of both the organizational advantages and the potential hazards of being a social group. Even though, in ecclesial groups we have a faith dimension that is often, though not always, lacking in other social or political groups, it is still important for us to continue to learn more and better ways of working, living, and planning, together. It is also necessary to understand some of the constraints of organizational life and how to manage them for our personal and corporate renewal.

D. Trends, Values, Norms, Climate, and a Process Approach to Change

Early in this section on individual and corporate renewal, we examined what are probably the two most important aspects of group life: 1.) systems theory and 2.) group climate theory. Trends, values, norms, and a process approach to change, must follow closely behind in importance. In fact, depending on the group, any one of these might assume first place in importance. I am sure that no one of these terms is new to readers, but it may be helpful to review these in the context of the corporate renewal of ecclesial groups, which is so essential to the implementation of the Decrees of the Second Vatican Council.

Trends:

A trend is a general tendency, a pattern of acting, or a recurring course of events. Trends may be the result of decisions to move a group in a certain direction or manner, or they may develop simply as a result of individual choices initiated by some and then imitated by others. No doubt, we have all been aware of the appearances of such trends.

Some trends are the results of societal change. All trends need to be examined, weighed and accepted or rejected by individuals and by groups. Trends may have a positive or a negative effect on the on-going life of groups and of individuals.

Positive trends are life-giving and authenticating for individuals and for groups. Positive trends contribute to the integrity and identity of groups and to their purpose and mission.

Negative trends, which produce results contrary to the declared values of a group, need to be challenged and even reversed. Negative trends, left unexamined and unchanged, can rob a group of its identity and integrity and thwart its effectiveness in mission.

It is commonly understood that trends in motion do not reverse themselves. Some clear, value-based decisions are required in groups in order to reverse or redirect trends when that is required for the integrity of a group.

From time to time it is important for a group leader to ask the members questions such as:

What trends do you observe among us? ... in the broader Church or society?
Which of these have positive potential in your opinion?
Which have negative potential in your opinion?
Which have both positive and negative effects?
Do the positive outweigh the negative if both effects are in evidence?
How might we, as a group, begin to examine and evaluate these trends?

Good beginning questions that might be used in evaluating trends in motion are:
What have been the best effects of this trend on our life and mission?
What have been some of the unfavorable effects of this trend on our life and mission?

Unexamined trends have the potential for rendering a group ineffective or dead.

Values:
Our values are known by the worth we assign to particular beliefs, experiences, activities, events, groups, and on and on ad infinitum. It is important that we clarify for ourselves individually and for ourselves as faith communities, just what our real values are so that from time to time we can examine our choices in light of those values. We must always distinguish between **espoused, experienced,** and **operative values.** Our espoused values are those that we say that we use to inform our choices. Our experienced values are those, which give us a sense of integrity or dissonance at the feeling level in their presence or absence, either as an individual or as a member of a group. Our operative values are those, which consistently inform and enable our choices and actions. Of course, all of these types of values have meaning and importance, but our operative values, if they are consistent with our faith beliefs and our personal and group integrity, are the ones that really contribute to our authenticity and renewal. Value-based choices are at the foundation of personal and corporate renewal. Some basic shared values are essential

to the on-going life of any group. A group that has no significant shared values cannot long remain a group.

Earlier it was stated that individual renewal and conversion is a challenging feat. It is easy to see that the corporate renewal and conversion of groups is an even more daunting task when one realizes that the life and mission of a group, especially an ecclesial group, must be rooted and grounded in a set of commonly held values. It is understandable that some values may vary from person to person. However, for a group to come into existence, there must to be an agreed upon common purpose and a set of commonly held values related to the purpose of the group. Major decisions must be made in light of these shared values. If we return to that basic unit of society and the basic unit of the Church, the family, we see the seedbed for a system of values. However, given the fact of the massive cultural shift of at least the last seventy years, we can see that forces well beyond the family are shaping value systems, and not only for the young. When we look at ecclesial groups: bishops' conferences, priests' senates, presbyterates, pastoral councils, religious orders and congregations, we see a distinct advantage. We have as our common value the Word of God in the Person of Jesus Christ, and in the sacred words found in Holy Scripture. In addition, we have two thousand years of Sacred Tradition as well as the formal challenges of the Councils of the Church, especially the most recent one, Vatican II. Even with such a strong value-based foundation, we must continue to form and reform our faith communities and our personal lives by examining our choices and actions to see that they are consistent with our espoused and operative values.

Values, like trends, can move into a group unannounced. From time to time we need to stop, to pray, and to examine the values and trends that may have inserted themselves into our mode of decision-making and living. Conversion, transformation, and an on-going process of renewal is a way of life for the Church and for all of its members in all of its ecclesial communities. Examined and confirmed trends and values play a major role in enabling this renewal.

Norms:

Norms are standards or patterns of accepted behavior in groups. Norms create the climate in a group.

The group climate is the general feeling tone that is a created by two factors:
1.) the quality of relationships between and among the members and,
2.) the clarity of purpose and a commitment to that purpose by the total group.

Norms can develop in a group as a matter of course, but if the group decides in advance which norms will be acceptable and which norms will not be acceptable, the probability of developing a life-giving group climate will be much higher.

Since norms create the climate in a group, and the climate, in large part, determines whether or not a group achieves its mission, it behooves us to learn to assess group norms. By doing this, we can strengthen those norms that are enabling and change those which are debilitating. As with values and trends, norms must be regularly examined to determine how they are enabling or blocking the purpose of a group or hindering the quality of life for the members. Norms are not always explicit; they are often implicit.

Some implicit negative norms that might develop in a group are:

"We have always done it that way."
"It is OK to be late." (No one ever comments.)
"Don't ask questions."
"I haven't tried it, but it won't work. (Uninformed veto)

Obviously, explicit positive norms, those agreed to by all of the members, would be more helpful in creating a purposeful climate, as well as a climate where every member feels valued and respected. Some explicit positive norms might be:

"We value each person's contributions."
"We examine multiple options before making a decision."
"We ask questions for clarification."
"Each person is accountable to the group."
"We challenge each other without attacking."

There is great value in declaring in advance the explicit norms that will be operative in a group.

There are two types of norms:
  Being norms – the quality of our personal presence to each other as individuals
  Doing norms– the quality of our corporate presence and contributions to the mission, task, or issue that confronts the group.

Climate:

In the world of weather, we know that winds, rain, temperature, and geographic location can all play a part in how we go about our daily tasks. There is a climate in human groups that is the product of the quality of relationships that exists between and among the members and the clarity and commitment that the members have in common regarding their primary purpose. Groups have to be formed, developed, reformed, and from time to time, renewed. Each time a group acquires one new member there is a new group, and the new member needs more than a simple introduction The first step in the formation of a group is to provide an opportunity for each member to share something of his/her personal life story as well as what hopes, fears, and expectations are brought to membership in the group. It is important that all members know, understand, and are committed to the expected norms and values commonly clarified and articulated by the membership. As strong and as clear as these factors in climate might be, it will be important from time to time for any group to assess its climate. One simple way to do this is to ask these questions:

How does it feel to be a member of this group?	(Feelings)	+ or -
What makes you feel this way?	(Behaviors)	+ or -
What <u>patterns</u> of behavior are allowed?	(Norms)	+ or -
What word describes the group climate?	(Climate)	+ or -

After allowing each person to respond to these questions, the group together will be able to name its climate and to decide if any changes in behavior and/or norms are needed to create a more productive climate. It is always important to focus on a sense of genuine community and a clear and strong commitment to the mission of the group.

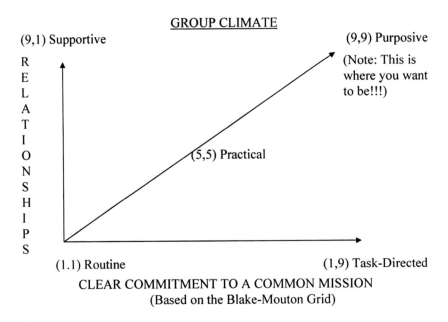

Process Approach to Change: A Method of Decision-Making in Groups

We are fast approaching the end of the section in this book entitled "Arch." Of the many enlightening and life-changing insights gleaned beyond the Arch, I would have to place The Corporate Reflection Process at the top of the list. Entering into a decision–making mode implies a need for change, growth, or renewal. One of the most common methods of decision-making in groups is that of voting. This inevitably concludes with winners and losers. There is a better way, and one that is especially suited to religious groups. How we make decisions will affect how the decisions are understood, accepted and implemented. How decisions are made will affect whether or not the fruits of these decisions will have a transforming effect in the lives of persons and groups. From my experience over a number of years with a variety of groups, I have found the Corporate Reflection Process to be highly effective in those groups willing to engage the process fully.

The Corporate Reflection Process is a highly collaborative method of decision-making. Each word in the title of this method has significant meaning. The word corporate implies a body or a group of bonded individuals. The word reflection implies a serious and prayerful consideration of the basic values and traditions of the group. Finally, process implies that the conclusion reached is the result of a gradual unfolding of the desired outcome. The description below will give two extreme styles of reaching decisions, those of power coercion and rationale empiricism. In between these two is the normative-re-educative model, a category to which the Corporate Reflection Process belongs.

TOLD   TRANSFORMED BY MUTUAL CHOICES   SOLD
(Power-coercion) (Normative re-education) (Rational empiricism)

In the first style, that of power-coercion, one person, or one group of persons with the proper authority, makes the decision and without further consultation, simply announces the decision.

At the other extreme, that of rational empiricism, one person or one group tries to give all of the reasons why a particular decision should be taken until argumentation prevails.

Between these two extremes, lies a mode of decision-making that begins with the group developing a set of normative criteria for reaching a particular decision. By the means of individual prayer, reflection, small group sharing, and integration of differences, a small group consensus is can be reached. The process then moves to a group-to-group dialogue where each small group's consensus (not individual preferences) forms the content for discussion, decision, and evaluation by the total group. By engaging in genuine dialogue the members are open to learning from one another and to growing in their mutual understanding of a common purpose. This method is most likely to engender commitment to decisions as well as to result in a deeper bonding among the members of the decision-making body. The Corporate Reflection Process enables both personal and corporate renewal and transformation. It is a process of mutual education and promotes a deeper understanding and commitment to decisions in a group. We have seen in this section that individual and corporate renewal, are mutually interactive, but that they engage the process of renewal differently. The process of personal renewal is one in which a person endeavors daily to take on the likeness of Christ through, prayer, sacraments, good works and the practice of the Christian virtues. The process of corporate renewal, in the context of the Christian faith community, at whatever level, is one in which a number of persons with a sense of common purpose, strive to reach goals that will further the mission of the Church in the world. Individual renewal practices will enhance a group, and group renewal efforts will contribute to individual growth and renewal in the life of the participating persons.

We have examined the organizational dimensions of all social systems, including those of the Church. In the Church we have the same subsystems as those to be found in any major organization or government structure: authority, maintenance, boundary, adaptive, and productive. We have identified the climate as the general feeling tone in a group, which develops as a result of the quality of relationships between and among the members of a group, and the clarity and commitment to the common purpose that is held by the members. Climate, more than any other single factor, determines the effectiveness of a group. Further, we saw that values, trends, and norms are present in all groups. It is vital that these are recognized, named, and periodically evaluated. Clearly defined and chosen values, trends, and norms will enhance the quality of a group's climate and its effectiveness in mission.

Serious efforts towards personal and corporate renewal are essential if ever we are to implement the documents of the Second Vatican Council. We have all been called to serious shared responsibility in assuming our rightful place in the Church. Together we are the Body of Christ. We are to preach by our lives the coming of the Reign of God. We can do this as individuals, but we have also been called to do this as a People. For this reason, it is vital that we grow in our understanding of differences between individual and corporate renewal and the importance of enabling their complementarities.

At this point I would like to share a thoughtful story and a brief confession. Very shortly after the close of the Second Vatican Council, I attended a lecture given by the General Superior of a major order of Catholic priests and brothers. He had attended the Vatican Council as an Observer. Toward the end of the lecture he said, "If anyone has not read all of the documents of the Second Vatican Council, at least twice, you have sinned grievously." There was a quiet titter in the hall. The speaker did not smile. He said further, "How can you call yourself Catholic if you do not even know what the Church teaches?" I have to confess that I have not read all of the documents twice, but I am hoping to have done so before I die.

E. *The Spirituality of Groups*

Before addressing the spirituality of groups, it is necessary to clarify the meaning of "spirituality," and the meaning of a "corporate person."

One very simple and straightforward definition of spirituality is that it is a style of life that flows from the presence of the Spirit of God within us. We could also say that Christian spirituality is the contemporary expression of Christian faith in the language of Christian living. It is the way we live who we are. Growing in the Christian spiritual life means growing in learning to express all aspects of your human and divine relationships in a way that reflects Christ.

A corporate person is a plurality of individuals who are in contact and in union with one another. In some instances the individuals are bonded to one another in a vowed life, for example, in marriage or by religious vows. They respond to one another and take each other into account. They are aware of significant commonalities, which bind them to one another. They believe that the whole body affects the individual and that the individual affects the whole body.

There are some clearly observable qualities that characterize both individuals and groups who are serious about the spiritual life:

+ There is openness to ongoing conversion and transformation,
+ There is a certain ability to stand alone, not as totally independent, but as having a clear sense of identity.
+ There is an awareness of God's presence and action in their lives, and in their history.
+ Such groups and persons have a tremendous capacity for carrying the pain of others.
+ There is a particular style of prayer that is integrated with life.
+ There is a high quality of personal presence to one another and to others in the wider society.
+ Groups that have entered into the transforming presence of the Spirit possess a power to challenge other social groups beyond themselves..
+ There is a willingness to learn and to engage in shared reflection leading to genuine dialogue.
+ There is a capacity for communal discernment toward shared decision-making.

+ A life-giving group climate is clearly in evidence.
+ These persons and groups are somehow noticeably "different."

This is captured in these words from Holy Scripture:

"Rather, living the truth in love, we should grow in every way into him who is head, Christ, from whom the whole body, joined and held together by every supporting ligament, with the proper functioning of each part, brings about the body's growth and builds itself up in love."[11]

Part II.
Steeples
1980 – 1992

Steeples have always been for me symbols of God's presence among us. I grew up, literally, in the shadow of the church where I was baptized. My religious vows, sometimes called a second baptism, were professed in a church with a magnificent steeple, which is not only the symbol of God's presence among us, but a symbol of the Congregation of Providence of which I am a member. That steeple is at the heart of our Motherhouse grounds, and is a constant reminder of our call to be ONE in union with God and with one another. In my ministry of working with religious congregations, dioceses, presbyterates, deaneries, parishes, colleges, and schools, I have been on site in many places throughout the United States, and in some parts of Canada, and Europe. Steeples in these places have been significant reminders of God's abiding presence among us. They are signs of our call to be a People, the People of God, reaching out to one another, and reaching out for God as the steeple reaches for the sky.

Part II. Steeples (1980-1992)
A. Reaching for God

In my introductory statement on steeples, I mentioned the church of my baptism and the church of my religious profession, Holy Trinity Church in New Albany, Indiana, and the Church of the Immaculate Conception at Saint Mary-of-the-Woods, Indiana. These are two of the many steeples that are significant religious symbols for me. Much of my Christian and religious life was spent in their shadow, and I should also say, in their light. In these places I was instructed, enlightened, and inspired by parents, family members, teachers, priests, and co-members of my religious community, regarding the importance of seeking God above all else. Steeples symbolize that seeking for me. The other steeples in my story will "rise" as we move ahead in the twelve-year period 1980-1992.

1980 was a very good year for two reasons: a new degree and a new assignment. In the spring of that year, as I was finishing a master's degree in spirituality at Saint Louis University, I received a telephone call that would result in my moving to a new arena for ministry. However, it turned out that this call would require that I continue to tap into the learning of the previous eight years. Again the timing factor entered the picture.

My degree in spirituality had provided me with training in individual spiritual direction. I was invited to Saint Meinrad College Seminary to be interviewed as a possible member of the Spiritual Formation Staff. After several days of interviews with representatives of the administration, the faculty, and the students, I was accepted for

1982 — With seminarians at Saint Meinrad

this assignment. I served as a spiritual director to college seminarians for four years. I want to say more about this, but before I do, a little story must be told about my first experience of the Saint Meinrad steeples.

From a distance one can see the twin steeples of the Saint Meinrad Archabbey Church. For the second time this view became one of the religious symbols on my journey of faith as it had during the days of our four years of group spiritual direction on the Cor Unum Renewal Team. Even though I wrote of the Cor Unum experience earlier, I wanted to save this story until now because it connects my two Saint Meinrad experiences. As we were finishing our initial training as a team in Saint Louis, Father Tom Swift, S.J., one of the "Two Prophets," called a meeting of all of the teams. He said, "It will be very important for you to have group spiritual direction. You will be living together, praying together, planning together, traveling together, and working together as a team. From time to time you need to meet with a spiritual director as a team. In that way you can review and assess how your community life and ministry are contributing to your personal and group spirituality." Those may not have been his exact words but that was the essence of his message. Prior to this meeting, each team was told to choose a coordinator. Our team had asked me to assume that role. At the end of that meeting Father Swift approached me saying, "I think your team should go to Saint Meinrad for spiritual direction. I have been watching what they are doing in that area and I think it would be a good place for your team." When we returned to

1972 — Fr. Aurelius, Spiritual Director for the Cor Unum Renewal Team

our Motherhouse, I told our General Superior about this. She called the Archabbot and made the arrangements. About every six weeks for the four years of the team's existence, we went either to Saint Meinrad, or our director, Father Aurelius Boberek, OSB, came to Saint Mary-of-the-Woods. I think the concept of group spiritual direction was a new one for us, but over time we came to understand and value the wise advice of Father Swift. It was essential that we would step back from our coast-to-coast travels and see just how we were living what we were trying to impart to others. Father Aurelius was a devoted listener and guide. As I tell this story, I am discovering over and over how the "arch" and "steeples" in my life keep re-appearing. So in mid-August of 1980, I moved to southern Indiana and found myself once again gazing upon the steeples of the Saint Meinrad Archabbey Church.

Coming from a family of six girls and no brothers, and having lived many years in the convent, it was quite a change to find myself in a college seminary atmosphere. The monks, faculty members, and students were very welcoming and I felt greatly at ease in the situation. The seminarians at that time represented about thirty-six dioceses from across the country. It was another great experience of the broader Church. I was impressed with the seriousness and sincerity of the young men who were in the process of testing their calls to the priesthood. It was a privilege to have been a companion to a number of them on their faith journeys. On occasion I am in touch with some of them. As I have mentioned several times in this memoir, in one way or another, most of my ministry assignments came to me unexpectedly. However, I can honestly say that each one seemed to have been a preparation for the next one.

At some point in my time at Saint Meinrad, a laywoman had been teaching a class entitled "Church Management" in the School of Theology. This was one of the required courses for students in the year prior to ordination. When the laywoman left the faculty, I was asked to take the class as I had had previous graduate work in administration. I agreed to take the class, but I asked to change the name of the course from "Church Management," to "Collaborative Relationships in the Church." I believe that the change in the course title was in greater harmony with the Church's new self-understanding as articulated in the decrees of Vatican Council II. It was important that future priests be well grounded in the principles of shared responsibility with the laity for the life and mission of the Church. While not diminishing the role of the authority of office held by a pastor, it required an understanding of the tripod of authority, which resides in the authority of office; the authority of personhood; and the authority of the faith community as a corporate person. No one of these can simply cancel any one of the others out. As we are so clearly taught by Saint Paul, "The eye cannot say to the hand, 'I do not need you,' nor again the head to the feet, 'I do not need you.' "[12]

During my years on the Formation Staff, one of my side assignments was that of advisor to a group called Cooperative Action for Community Development, or CACD. This was an outreach program to meet the needs of people in the area who were living well below the poverty line. I can remember, in particular, a seminarian coming into my office after one of his visits to a home not too far from the seminary. He walked into the office with something of a shocked expression. He had just visited a family whose "house" had a dirt floor. I have wondered if that experience during his time of priestly formation has had a fruitful impact on his awareness of the People of God as the Body of Christ. He was truly moved and concerned at the sight of that destitute family. I hope that this awareness and concern has carried on into his later life. Since those days, it has occurred to me that the name of that program, Cooperative Action for Community Development, is an apt description of the Church itself. We are called to work together to build up the Mystical Body of Christ, the Church. This requires more than providing material sustenance, but also being a source of love and mutual support on our common journey of faith called life.

I truly enjoyed my time at the seminary. I was encouraged and inspired by the generous young men who were testing their calls to priesthood. Little did I realize that this time was a preparation for me to move out into the broader Church. With one more year on my contract, it seemed that God was intervening again. I received a visit from the Chancellor of the Archdiocese of Indianapolis, who presented me with a request from the Archbishop to open a new archdiocesan office. I, in turn, presented it to the President-Rector. This was once again, a proposed change that was neither sought nor expected, but by this time I had caught on to a pattern that was emerging in my ministerial life. It seemed to say to me, "Go with the flow. Follow the movement of the Spirit." After a discussion with the President-Rector, and with my

Provincial Superior, it was agreed that I should take the position that was about to be established in the archdiocese.

So, in 1984, Archbishop O'Meara asked me to open the Office for Pastoral Councils. I received a one-page job description, which stated basically, "Strengthen parish pastoral councils where they exist; establish them where they do not exist. Form deanery pastoral councils and an archdiocesan pastoral council." There had never been deanery councils, or an archdiocesan council. That one-page job description was an eight-year assignment. My four years in the seminary were a good preparation for being thrust into the life of the local Church in a new way. So when I left the steeples of the Archabbey Church of Saint Meinrad, I moved around the cluster of steeples in the thirty-nine counties of the Archdiocese of Indianapolis.

Prior to the opening of the Office for Pastoral Councils many parishes had what were termed simply, "Parish Councils." Happily, the Archbishop had used the term, "Pastoral," which had been stressed in the Vatican Council documents to describe the office. The distinction, "pastoral," made it clear that the purpose of the councils was more than taking care of the buildings and finances. They were to be truly "pastoral" in nature and purpose, that is, to assist the pastors, deans, bishops, and archbishops in promoting the spiritual well-being of the members as individuals and as a community of believers. In working with these councils I met the living Church in a new way. I experienced among the people of the archdiocese the same kind of sincerity and seriousness that I had experienced with the young seminarians. Here and there one would occasionally meet with resistance or lethargy, but on the whole, people were ready to assume their rightful place in the Church. They saw clearly that "going" to Church was not enough; they were called to "be" the Church. This would require more of them, and they seemed to me to be ready for the challenge.

B. Structures - A Means of Growth and Renewal

People come together to be and to do what they could never be and do alone. When these gatherings become formalized, new structures have arisen. Even in the early Church, in the days after Pentecost, new believers formed themselves into communities with structures and a variety of functions. As time went on, other Christians gathered in monastic communities, and later in the active apostolic communities of women and men. They believed that they could pursue the Christian life more intensely together and find support, not only in the example and encouragement of one another, but in the very structures that brought them together as a community. One structure was simply the daily time schedule for prayer, celebration of the Eucharist, community meetings and other regular events. Over time, this mutuality of lifestyle had the potential for calling each member to a deeper and more intense living of the Christian way of life. Then there came a time when the numbers grew to the extent that these communities needed other more formal structures as we shall see.

The very word, "structure," has a rigid sound to it. However, its purpose is not rigid. It is to provide a way for persons to come together, not only for the group itself, and the individual members in it, but for a purpose beyond the group. In the Church, that means for the sanctification, evangelization, and transformation of the members as well as of the world beyond.

Rather than beginning at the universal level of structures, let us begin by looking at one of the smallest official ecclesial structures, the deanery, the middle structure between the diocese and the parish. I choose to focus on the deanery since the council structure at that level is less well understood and utilized

As the Catholic Church grew and spread throughout the world, dioceses were formed, made up of defined territories with subdivisions called parishes. Later clusters of parishes were formed and given the name vicariates forane or deaneries. This middle structure between the diocese and the parish had the potential for collaboration between and among parishes. Where used to best advantage, parishes within a given deanery could share ideas, resources, and personnel. The parishes could also be a support and an inspiration to one another, just as individuals within a faith community could do this for one another. As I mentioned at the end of the last section, my job description of 1984 included the establishment of deanery pastoral councils in the Archdiocese of Indianapolis. Prior to that time these councils did not exist in the archdiocese. From my experience of working with persons having a position similar to mine, I learned that the use of this middle structure of councils was rather uncommon. After consulting with a specialist in organizational planning, I was encouraged to try to strengthen the deanery structure. A gap between the central governance of the archdiocese and the local parishes was organizationally, a weakness. It may be helpful here to include some documentation from the <u>Deanery Pastoral Council Guidelines of the Archdiocese of Indianapolis</u>. This document was developed by our newly established office.

Deanery

In order to move toward a common understanding of the role of the Deanery Pastoral Councils, it is necessary to clarify the meaning and purpose of the Deanery. The following statements can assist us in this clarification:

> "In order to foster pastoral care through common action, several neighboring parishes can be joined together into special groups such as vicariates forane (deaneries)" <u>Canon 374</u>

> "The bishop attaches much importance to the boundary arrangements of these groupings, and to their proper and effective functioning, for they contribute much to concerted pastoral action and are a necessary means of subsidiarity and to a good distribution of ministry throughout the diocese." <u>(Directory on the Pastoral Ministry of Bishops) 1973.</u>

Deanery Pastoral Council

The Deanery Pastoral Council forms with the Dean, a leadership body whose primary concern is that of calling parishes in the Deanery out of parochialism and into more effective collaboration in order to further the Church's mission in a given Deanery.

The Deanery Council serves as an intermediate archdiocesan structure for the purpose of communication and collaborative pastoral planning between and among parishes within a given deanery; between and among deaneries, and between deaneries and the Archdiocesan Pastoral Council. The Deanery, as a middle structure, is essential to effective Church management, standing as it does, between the basic unit of the parish and the larger systemic unit of the archdiocese.

Council Spirituality

Following the example of Jesus, the members of the Deanery Pastoral Council will turn again and again to prayer, seeking guidance and direction from the Holy Spirit in all of their deliberations and actions. The shared faith of Council members, their mutual concern and Christian charity, the energizing effect of each other's apostolic zeal, combine to create a climate for spiritual growth.

A Deanery Pastoral Council which develops a sense of identity and mission will serve as a leaven of renewal for its own members as well as for the faith communities within the Deanery.

Dean – Deanery Pastoral Council

The quality of the relationships, which develops between the Dean and the Deanery Pastoral Council, ought to be the fruit of prayer, open and respectful dialogue, and a shared understanding of the distinct but complementary roles of Dean and Council. The Council is in a consultative relationship with the Dean, sharing decisions, which contribute to fostering collaboration among parishes in the Deanery. A true spirit of mutuality and collaboration ought to be the hallmark of the relationship between the Dean and the Deanery Pastoral Council.[13]

Much of what has been said here in regard to deaneries can be said also regarding the structures above and below the deaneries, that is, the diocese/archdiocese and the parish. The roles and relationships between the councils at the parish level and their pastors, and councils at the archdiocesan or diocesan level and their archbishops or bishops must be clearly understood and developed. No doubt, one of the most difficult concepts to grasp is that of shared responsibility in the Church. That is more than a "catch phrase." In his commentary on the Dogmatic Constitution on the Church, Cardinal Avery Dulles, S.J. stated:

"...The Constitution devotes an entire chapter to the description of the Church as the 'new People of God'. This title, solidly founded in Scripture, met a profound desire of the Council to put greater emphasis on the human and communal side of the Church, rather than on the institutional and hierarchical aspects, which have sometimes been overstressed in the past. ... While everything said about the 'People of God' as a whole is applicable to the laity, it should not be forgotten that the term 'People of God' refers to the total community of the Church, including the pastors as well as the other faithful."[14]

It requires understanding what was spoken of earlier as the tripod of authority, 1.) authority of office, 2.) authority of personhood 3.) authority of the community as a corporate person. Each has the right and the obligation to "author" or to initiate content and insights that would contribute to a shared decision. Those with the office of authority and the council members must be willing to engage in genuine dialogue toward decisions. It may be helpful to look at the concept of dialogue and to its practical application.

Dialogue

In my eight years (1984-1992) of working with parish, deanery and archdiocesan councils, a word that became very sacred to me was that of dialogue. One of the most profound descriptions of dialogue that I have come across is this one:

> "Dialogue is to love
> what blood is to the body.
> When the flow of blood stops,
> the body dies.
> When dialogue stops,
> love dies
> and resentment is born.
> But dialogue
> can restore a dead relationship.
> Indeed, this is the miracle of dialogue.
> It can bring a relationship into being,
> and it can bring into being

> once again
> a relationship that had died."¹⁵

To quote the "prophet" Father Tom Swift, S.J., "Dialogue is an encounter with <u>who we are in those who are unlike us</u>. Dialogue is a synthesis of divergent views under a unifying concept." He held that the prerequisites for genuine dialogue were: personal presence, mutual respect, and a willingness to be influenced by new information and insights.

In working with councils and other ecclesial structures I often placed these "Hoped-for Outcomes from Dialogue" before the groups. These statements seemed to engage and inspire persons to enter into a dialogic relationship.

- Shared vision and commitment to a common mission
- Mutual support in working toward the realization of the mission
- Decisions that will embody the aspirations and insights of all the members
- Informed decision-making – informed in the deepest philosophical sense, that is, embodying the lived experience of the members as well as the empirical data
- A bonding in faith and love among the members as a result of increased knowledge and understanding of one another
- An increased willingness to call and to be called to greater fidelity and accountability.

Dialogue requires a high quality of personal presence, mutual respect, and an openness to new information and ideas. It cannot be an instrument of personal growth and quality shared decision-making in groups where the normal mode of communication is that of shooting darts of privatized wisdom at one another. Genuine dialogue demonstrates an ability to listen not only to words and ideas, but to listen for feelings, values, and understandings. To be in a dialogic relationship with one or more persons is to demonstrate a willingness to be influenced or to change when one's own truth is obviously incomplete. There is a willingness to call or to be called beyond our current state or position. Without this openness, we set it up to encourage each other to mediocrity. In dialogue, each one's truth is presented peacefully with neither capitulation nor domination. Everyone who participates feels valued and important.

When councils at the parish, deanery or diocesan/archdiocesan levels come together as genuine faith communities and carry on their primary task of pastoral planning in a dialogic manner, the Church is truly alive and well. In those groups, the genuine shared responsibility and collaboration called for by the Second Vatican Council has become a reality. This mode of operation in the Church often requires all three aspects of authority to he exercised in a new way. The one holding the authority of office recognizes the need to be attentive to the authority of each person by right of personhood and membership in the Church, and then to recognize the authority of the council as a corporate person. While strictly speaking the office of authority holds ultimate responsibility, councils can be experienced as more than simply consultative. Decisions should result in a tapestry of the prayerful reflection, wisdom, insights, and desires of all three sources of authority. This will certainly enhance the quality of the decisions made, as well as the potential for commitment to those decisions.

We have been examining some of the structures for growth and renewal in the smaller sub-units of the Church, let us now look at the structure of the Church as a whole, by examining the Ecumenical Council. The following statement from "The Dogmatic Constitution on the Church" issuing from the Second Vatican Council describes the Universal Church as a social structure:

> "The one mediator, Christ, established and ever sustains here on earth his holy Church the community of faith, hope and charity, as a visible organization, through which He communicates truth and grace to all. But the society structured with hierarchical organs and the Mystical Body of Christ, the visible society and the spiritual community, the earthly Church and the Church endowed with heavenly riches, are not to be thought of as two realties. On the contrary, they form one complex reality, which comes together from a human and a divine element. For this reason the Church is compared, not without significance, to the mystery of the Incarnate Word. As the assumed nature inseparably united to him, serves the Divine Word as a living organism, so in a somewhat similar way, does the communal

structure of the Church serve the Spirit of Christ who vivifies it in the building up of the body." (cf. Eph. 4:156)[16]

The twenty-first Ecumenical Council, Vatican Council II, stands out as a structure with the potential for bringing new life and vigor to the Church. This Council was the first to be called in over one hundred years and it was unique in the history of the Church. The more than 2,300 bishops who attended were, for the most part, natives of their own countries, not missionary bishops. They understood well the needs of their own dioceses. Modern means of travel allowed, for the first time, a Council at this level to be truly representative of the Universal Church. Obviously, the Church does not exist for itself. As you read in the introductory part of this book in the outline, "Themes of the Second Vatican Council," seven of the sixteen documents, that is, almost half, addressed the mission of the Church to those outside its membership. In his opening address on October 11, 1962, Pope John XXIII made it clear that this Council would be different. He said, "The substance of the ancient doctrine of the deposit of faith is one thing, and the way in which it is presented is another. And it is the latter that must be taken into great consideration with patience, if necessary, everything being measured in the forms and proportions of a Magisterium, (official church teaching) which is predominantly pastoral in character."[17] And to spell this out further, he goes on to say, " … the Catholic Church, raising the torch of religious truth by means of this Ecumenical Council, desires to show herself to be the loving mother of all, benign, patient, full of mercy and goodness toward (all) who are separated from her."[18] The Council was to be truly a pastoral council and one that was genuinely ecumenical. It was not to be a Council, "concerned only with antiquity."[19] In another place in this monumental opening address, Pope John XXIII summed up the pastoral nature of the Council by saying, "The salient point of this Council is not, therefore, a discussion of one article or another of the fundamental doctrine of the Church which has repeatedly been taught by the Fathers and by ancient and modern theologians, and which is presumed to be well known and familiar to all. For this a Council is not necessary."[20]

C. Bringing Structures to Life

In the opening sentence in the section on "Structures - A Means of Growth and Renewal," I made this statement: "People come together to be and to do what they cannot be and do alone." Structures, in and of themselves, are lifeless forms. The people within them can bring them to life, but that can happen only if the members are willing to take the time to learn the basic factors of group formation, development, and renewal. These were presented in the first section of this book under these titles:

> Individual and Corporate Renewal
> Trends, Values, Norms, Climate
> A Process Approach to Change
> The Spirituality of Groups

Of course, having understood these elements of group life, the key to success in realizing the purpose of a group is to have a commitment to a clear, shared vision and mission. We need to ask: "Why have we come together? What are we called to be and to do?" In the various sub-structures of the Universal Church, the overall vision and mission will be that of the evangelization and transformation of the world. However, in any one of those same sub-structures, say a presbyterate or a priests' senate, the vision and mission may have to be more particularized, but always mindful of the larger vision and mission of the Church. This would be true also in the multiple sub-structures of the Church such as diocesan offices, commissions, or committees. Then we can move beyond the formal ecclesial structures of a local Church to some of the other supportive entities of schools, seminaries, colleges, universities, hospitals, and social services, to name a few. In each of these there are multiple structures set up to further the specific mission of the institution in light of the larger mission of the Church. Just how life-giving each of these groups is for its individual members and just how effective it is in realizing its purpose, will determine its potential for realizing the specific and overall mission.

Religious communities of women and men have been engaging in the same effort of renewing their structures in order to bring about the collaborative and fully participative mode of operation encouraged by the

Second Vatican Council. It has been my distinct privilege to have served in a facilitative role with many of these groups.

On the pages immediately following this one, I would like to share the contents of a session I conducted for a Bishop and his Presbyterate in the Midwest. This is the kind of experience that is needed to help such a group move through the changing pastoral context from 60's and beyond.

In calling the Church to a stronger pastoral presence in the world, the Second Vatican Council set the stage for a shift in the use of structures and modes of interaction between and among the members of the Church, clerical, lay, and religious. This is not to say that the call was clearly heard and understood by all. In some places and in some hearts, it was heard but misunderstood or unheeded. The current resurgence of concern and interest in re-examining this call to conversion and renewal according to the teachings of the Council is a sign of hope. For the hopes and calls of the Council to be more fully realized, every baptized Catholic, ordained or non-ordained, may have to engage in some serious study, and a conversion of personal styles of responsible action and interaction. A simple review of the changing pastoral context, beginning with the 1960's and moving through to the new Millennium and beyond, may be one way to understand this need and to respond to it.

Changing Pastoral Context

1960	1972	1984	1996	2008--
Bureaucratic	Therapeutic	Participative	Collaborative	
Emphasis on Roles	Emphasis on Personal Need	Effort to Blend the Good of the Individual with the Common Good	Pastoral Context for a Genuine Mutuality The Church as a People of Mission	

Marie Kevin Tighe, S.P.

QUALITY OF PERSONAL PRESENCE

A. Attentiveness

B. Questioning for Understanding

C. Responding

D. Committed Response

E. Call

"The fact that most people spend a good part of their lives maintaining social roles may tempt us to confuse these roles with their personal identities."
        Regis Duffy, O.F.M.
        <u>Real Presence</u>

To be present is <u>to be there</u> for another and to allow the other <u>to be there</u> for you.

"What is most personal and unique in each of us is probably the very element which would, if it were shared or expressed, speak most deeply to others."
        Carl Rogers
        <u>On Becoming a Person</u>

QUALITY OF PERSONAL PRESENCE

A. Unconditional Acceptance

B. Creative Communication

C. Creative Confrontation

Arch, Steeples, and Dome

DIALOGUE TOWARD MUTUALITY

Characteristics of Dialogue:

A. Demonstrates an ability to listen not only to words and ideas, but to listen for feeling, values and understanding

B. Presupposes some common base of mutuality, some common ground

C. Exhibits reverence for differences in persons' insights and experiences

D. Embodies shared reflection moving toward a shared vision

E. Demonstrates a willingness to be influenced or to change when one's own truth is obviously incomplete; an openness to mutual influence, that is, a willingness to call and to be called (Without such openness we set it up to encourage each other to mediocrity)

F. Each one's truth is presented peacefully with neither capitulation nor domination

G. Everyone who participates feels valued and important

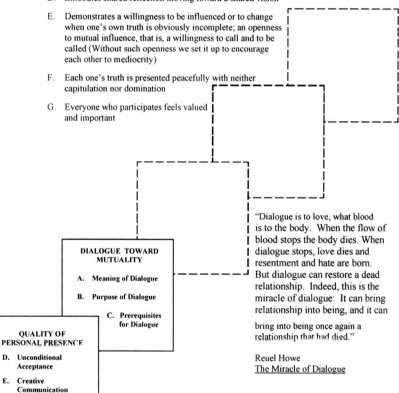

"Dialogue is to love, what blood is to the body. When the flow of blood stops the body dies. When dialogue stops, love dies and resentment and hate are born. But dialogue can restore a dead relationship. Indeed, this is the miracle of dialogue: It can bring relationship into being, and it can bring into being once again a relationship that had died."

Reuel Howe
The Miracle of Dialogue

DIALOGUE TOWARD MUTUALITY

A. Meaning of Dialogue
B. Purpose of Dialogue
C. Prerequisites for Dialogue

QUALITY OF PERSONAL PRESENCE

D. Unconditional Acceptance
E. Creative Communication
F. Creative Confrontation

Marie Kevin Tighe, S.P.

TOWARD A SHARED VISION AND COLLABORATIVE MISSION

A. The Presbyterate is a key corporate entity within the diocese. It has a clear group identity, and from time to time must assess its integrity and effectiveness in pursuing a common vision and mission

B. What would we like to see in our Presbyterate as we move forward in the 90's and beyond?

FOR REFLECTION:

Canon 265: "Every cleric must be incardinated into some particular church or personal prelature or into an institute of consecrated life or society endowed with this faculty, so that unattached or transient clerics are not allowed at all."

Canon 275: "Since they all work toward one end, the building up of the Body of Christ, clerics are to be united among themselves by the bond of brotherhood and prayer; they are to strive for cooperation among themselves in accord with the prescriptions of particular law."

Revised
Code of Canon Law
1983

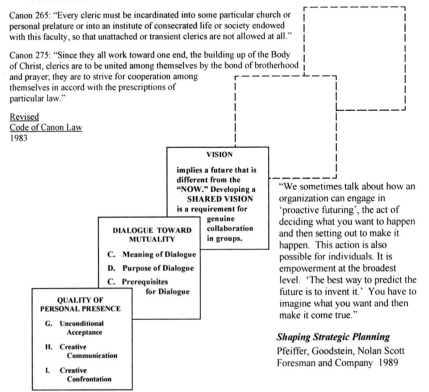

VISION

implies a future that is different from the "NOW." Developing a **SHARED VISION** is a requirement for genuine collaboration in groups.

DIALOGUE TOWARD MUTUALITY

C. Meaning of Dialogue
D. Purpose of Dialogue
C. Prerequisites for Dialogue

QUALITY OF PERSONAL PRESENCE

G. Unconditional Acceptance
H. Creative Communication
I. Creative Confrontation

"We sometimes talk about how an organization can engage in 'proactive futuring', the act of deciding what you want to happen and then setting out to make it happen. This action is also possible for individuals. It is empowerment at the broadest level. 'The best way to predict the future is to invent it.' You have to imagine what you want and then make it come true."

Shaping Strategic Planning
Pfeiffer, Goodstein, Nolan Scott
Foresman and Company 1989

MANY VOICES — ONE WORD
Moving Toward Consensus

Consensus is not based on statistics alone, i.e. averaging individual answers.

Consensus does not rely on numbers, i.e. the majority is correct.

Unanimity is not required for consensus.

What is required is:

- that everyone has had a chance to express an opinion
- that everyone has had the opportunity to examine the opinions of others and to clarify the thinking and the facts behind them
- that each one is able to be committed to the group's answer, knowing that the probabilities are high that the group response is at least as "right" as his individual answer

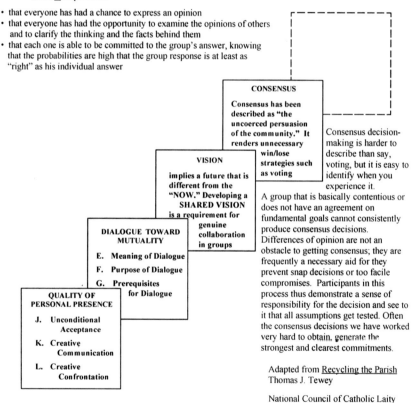

CONSENSUS

Consensus has been described as "the uncoerced persuasion of the community." It renders unnecessary win/lose strategies such as voting

VISION

implies a future that is different from the "NOW." Developing a SHARED VISION is a requirement for genuine collaboration in groups

DIALOGUE TOWARD MUTUALITY

E. Meaning of Dialogue
F. Purpose of Dialogue
G. Prerequisites for Dialogue

QUALITY OF PERSONAL PRESENCE

J. Unconditional Acceptance
K. Creative Communication
L. Creative Confrontation

Consensus decision-making is harder to describe than say, voting, but it is easy to identify when you experience it. A group that is basically contentious or does not have an agreement on fundamental goals cannot consistently produce consensus decisions. Differences of opinion are not an obstacle to getting consensus; they are frequently a necessary aid for they prevent snap decisions or too facile compromises. Participants in this process thus demonstrate a sense of responsibility for the decision and see to it that all assumptions get tested. Often the consensus decisions we have worked very hard to obtain, generate the strongest and clearest commitments.

Adapted from <u>Recycling the Parish</u>
Thomas J. Tewey

National Council of Catholic Laity

Marie Kevin Tighe, S.P.

NAMING THE FUTURE TOGETHER

Shaping our corporate life:
A Plan for the Renewal of Our Presbyterate

Power Coercion	Normative Re-education	Rational Empiricism
(EXTREME)	(CONVERSION)	(EXTREME)
	(CHANGE OF HEART)	

<u>Integrative change</u> produces growth, renewal, conversion for individuals and for groups

<u>Additive change</u> imposed from the outside is burdensome. It may result in conformity to external forces, but it seldom produces genuine growth, renewal or a change of heart.

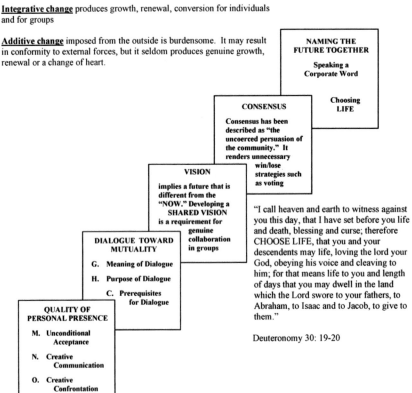

NAMING THE FUTURE TOGETHER
Speaking a Corporate Word
Choosing LIFE

CONSENSUS
Consensus has been described as "the uncoerced persuasion of the community." It renders unnecessary win/lose strategies such as voting

VISION
implies a future that is different from the "NOW." Developing a SHARED VISION is a requirement for genuine collaboration in groups

DIALOGUE TOWARD MUTUALITY
G. Meaning of Dialogue
H. Purpose of Dialogue
C. Prerequisites for Dialogue

QUALITY OF PERSONAL PRESENCE
M. Unconditional Acceptance
N. Creative Communication
O. Creative Confrontation

"I call heaven and earth to witness against you this day, that I have set before you life and death, blessing and curse; therefore CHOOSE LIFE, that you and your descendants may life, loving the lord your God, obeying his voice and cleaving to him; for that means life to you and length of days that you may dwell in the land which the Lord swore to your fathers, to Abraham, to Isaac and to Jacob, to give to them."

Deuteronomy 30: 19-20

The end result of the three-day convocation with this Presbyterate was the development of a vision statement to give focus to the priests regarding their common mission. The major goal of this time together was to strengthen the bond of mutuality in the group and thus to strengthen each priest for his life of ministry with and among God's People.

This is the statement:

Vision Statement

- By the power of God, we want the Presbyterate of this Local Church to be men who:

- have a strong identity an ministers of Jesus Christ.

- are committed to a relationship of collaboration with the Bishop in a manner that is life-giving to both the Bishop and the Priests as we pursue our common mission.

- are committed to a relationship of collaboration with the laity, taking seriously our complementary roles in pursuing the common mission of the Church.

- are attentive to the movement of the Spirit among them, men who pray together and call each other to ongoing conversion.

- as members of one body, we really care for each other and are committed to each other.

- reach out to each other when in pain or alienation, and respect each other despite difference in style, background, or theological persuasion, and whose members concretely live out and grow in this vision.

D. Widening Circles of Church

In this section of the book on "Steeples," and on this current topic of "Widening Circles of Church," I return to the church of my baptism and the other sacraments of initiation. My parish church was almost next door to our home. The side living room window gave us a full view of people coming and going to church. The bells in its steeple were frequently ringing. In those early days I thought of the church as a building and as a place to go for Mass. It was some time later that I began to understand that we were called to "be" the Church, and that our identity was to be one with Jesus as the Mystical Body. In the Dogmatic Constitution on the Church of the Second Vatican Council we read:

> "For by communicating his Spirit, Christ mystically constitutes as his body, those brothers (and sisters) of his who are called together from every nation."[21]

As I moved into the next circle of the Church, I found myself on the motherhouse grounds of the Sisters of Providence of Saint Mary-of-the-Woods. I was there to begin my remote preparation for committing myself to a deeper union with God and to the mission and ministry of the Church as a member of this religious community. The steeple of the conventual church there is modeled on the Church of the Trinité in Paris, an appropriate reminder of our community's French roots. That steeple was a first, but at the time an unknown indicator, of how wide my circle of Church would become over the years. But even at this point, I was aspiring to become a member of a community with a membership spread from coast to coast in the United States and in Taiwan. In 1920, the Sisters of Providence widened their "circle of Church," challenging them to send the first American sisters to the mainland of China.

My first teaching assignment after my profession of vows was in the Archdiocese of Chicago, the largest archdiocese in the Midwest both then and now. The parish to which I was assigned was predominately Polish. This nationality was new to me, but the strong witness of this group to the Catholic faith again stretched my awareness of the universality of the Church. The next twenty-eight years were spent as teacher, principal and provincial council member, chiefly in the state of Indiana and in the Archdiocese of Indianapolis. I realize now, more in retrospect than I did at that time, how much I experienced the Church as the "People of God." In the various places where I ministered, I experienced people living out the "Universal Call to Holiness" made by the Council.

> "It is quite clear that all Christians in any state or walk of life are called to the fullness of Christian life and to the perfection of love, and by this holiness a more human manner of life is fostered also in earthly society."[22]

In the years 1972-1980, covered in the section called "The Arch," I experienced the Church across the country in working for corporate renewal in more than thirty congregations, as well as in our own. Each of these experiences intensified my awareness, not just of the geographic spread of the Church, but of the many living witnesses of the Gospel message among God's People.

For me, this seems an appropriate place to give recognition to our SP Corporate Renewal Team. I say this at this point in my memoir because we were, in a sense, a "mini- Church." We chose the name Cor Unum. Where there is one heart there is one body. Yes, there was one body but six members. Sister Marie Clarice Toomey was the eldest, a former provincial and a woman of grace and dignity, one who could calm the concerns of her age group and be a calming presence for all of us. I came next in age and was chosen by the team as coordinator, assigned to call the group to planning sessions and to oversee our mission to the Congregation. Sister Rosemary Rafter was next in age, a gentle and organized member who had a way of seeking out those who might be struggling with learning new modes of "being" in dialogic relationships. Sister Grace Marie Meehan was next in line, a delightful Irish lass, (not far ahead of that in age!) Her cheerful disposition added to her facilitative skills. To her other duties was added that of "chief of transportation," in planning our trips around the country. Sister Joan Matthews was another cheerful and light-hearted member, who, while taking our mission seriously and contributing greatly to it, kept our spirits up with her music and laughter. The youngest member was in her twenties, Sister Mary Beth Klingel. Her youth and enthusiasm, along with her exceptional organizational skills, helped to keep us on track. Her presence gave us credibility with the younger members of the community. I believe it was the unity of the Cor Unum Team, and our commitment to the Church and to our Congregation of the Sisters of Providence, that kept our spirits alive during those difficult years of renewal. I believe that our common prayer, our regular group spiritual direction, our community life, and shared vision and mission, allowed us to be truly, a microcosm of the Church. And yet, each of us had her circles of the Church widened as we worked across diocesan lines with our sisters around the country. Our task of initiating this process of corporate renewal in our Congregation ended in 1976.

In 1980 my circle "widened" again! This time I was asked to facilitate a General Chapter for an international community of sisters. The Chapter was to take place in Rome. This was to be my first trip abroad and happily it would take me to the "headquarters" of the Catholic Church. However, on my way to the Eternal City, I had an experience that placed me in another wider circle of the Church! One of our sisters, Sister Ruth Ellen Doane, was teaching in Dusseldorf, Germany at that time, and someone had given her an extra ticket for the Oberammergau Passion Play. Participating in that moving spectacle was a never-to-be-forgotten experience. Over and above the power of the performance, was the experience of sitting in the midst of persons of every race, and I am certain, of every creed. Each one was following the text with a libretto of her or his, own language. It was truly an experience of the universality of Christendom, and of the love and mercy of God for all peoples.

After this wonderful spiritual experience, I boarded a train in southern Germany and traveled southward toward the Eternal City. I arrived in Rome on June 26. On June 29, we celebrated the Feast of Saints Peter and Paul. That is one of the few days when the Pope celebrates Mass at the main altar of the basilica. The sisters who had invited me, had graciously obtained a ticket for me to be seated in the main transept of the basilica. Here again, as at the Passion play, I found myself surrounded by the Church Universal, not the building, but the People of God. When I approached the altar to receive Holy Communion, the minister was one of the Benedictine monks of Saint Meinrad Archabbey in southern Indiana. This was a surprising and fortuitous happening, since upon my return to Indiana, I would begin another "circle widening" at Saint Meinrad Seminary, where young men from around the country were preparing for the priesthood.

The participants in the General Chapter were predominately from English or Portuguese-speaking countries. The main task of the delegates was to approve their revised Constitutions. The preliminary revision had taken place, but Chapter approval was necessary. We began by developing a set of common criteria for evaluation. Happily, the language groups were evenly divided numerically, with thirty sisters in each group. In the morning they met in ten groups of six members each; five groups in English and five groups in Portuguese. In that way the dialogue moved more easily. In the afternoon, with the help of simultaneous translations, the entire group heard the results of all of the morning sessions. In the end, this group achieved unanimous agreement. The key to this approach to decision-making is a commitment of time and the use of a disciplined process. I commend the Religious of the Sacred Hearts of Jesus and Mary for the way in which they engaged this process. I had to leave the Chapter two days before it ended because of being about to begin a new assignment. Upon my arrival home I received a message from the General Superior in Rome, saying, "Constitutions unanimously approved!" That was the fruit of genuine corporate reflection and dialogue.

The period of time in this section on "Widening Circles of Church" covers the years 1980-1992. During that time, in addition to my one-month assignment in Rome, I spent four years as spiritual director at Saint Meinrad Seminary and eight years as Director of the Office for Pastoral Councils in Indianapolis. In all of these instances, I felt that I was at the heart of the Church. That has been the case since my earliest days as a member of the domestic church of the Tighe Family. From that point on, the circles began to widen and wherever I find myself there is always an awareness that I do not stand alone. Each of us is called to be one with God and one with each other. These words from Lumen Gentium confirm this fact for me.

> "All are called to belong to the new People of God. This People therefore, while remaining one and only one, is to be spread throughout the whole world and to all ages in order that the design of God's will be fulfilled. He made human nature one in the beginning and has decreed that all his children who were scattered should be finally gathered together as one."[23]

E. Called to Be the Church in a New Way

No place in the documents of the Second Vatican Council will you find the actual words used in the title of this section. However, for those who lived in the Church before the Council and who are still living now, and who have, at least to some extent, internalized the teachings that came from the Council, there is a sense of "newness." Words that are often used to describe the Council are "renewal, change of scope, development of doctrine, the spirit of the Council, collegiality, shared responsibility, adaptation, the age of the laity," to name but a few characteristics. The fact that two of the four major documents went to great lengths to speak to the world about the life and mission of the Church, implies that in a period of time in the secular world marked by radical change, the Church needed to adapt, renew, and clarify its presence and role both to the members of the Church and to those outside the Church.

For me personally, I can say that the newness was a deeper realization that the Church was not "something" outside myself. I understood in a much more profound way, the reality of being a member of the Mystical Body of Christ. In some way I was to make God's presence known and experienced by those with whom I lived and ministered. I am not sure that that was always the case, but this deeper realization gave a renewed meaning to my life. The path that was opened to me in the post-Conciliar years was not one that I had mapped out for myself. Each new assignment enabled me to live and to promote what the Second Vatican Council called us to be and to do as Church. Telling that story was my motivation for writing this memoir. The Council's documents will remain dead letters unless we call one another to learn the ways of dialogue, collaboration and mutuality in fulfilling the mission entrusted to us as the Church.

In the very first article of the first document of the Council, that of the Constitution on the Sacred Liturgy, we read:

> The sacred Council has set out to impart an everlasting vigor to the Christian life of the faithful; to adapt more closely to the needs of our age those institutions, which are subject to change; to foster whatever can promote union among all who believe in Christ; to strengthen whatever can help to call all (hu)mankind into the Church's fold. Accordingly, it sees particularly

cogent reasons for undertaking the reform and promotion of the liturgy."[24]

So, at the outset, there was a "hint" that the world reality was calling the Church, not to dismantle its core identity and purpose, but to call itself to a greater sense of communion within itself and with the larger world. Both in the Dogmatic Constitution on the Church and in the Decree on the Laity, numerous articles stress the importance of the laity in the furthering of the official mission of the Church, to make God known and loved, and to love and serve one another in God's name. While the Council reiterated the hierarchical nature of the Church, this gathering stressed the role of the laity in ways that were genuinely new and different. One of the strongest and clearest statements to this effect is the following:

> "Though they differ essentially and not only in degree, the common priesthood of the faithful and the ministerial or hierarchical priesthood are none the less ordered to one another; each in its own proper way shares in the one priesthood of Christ. The ministerial priest, by the sacred power that he has, forms and rules the priestly people. In the person of Christ, he effects the eucharistic sacrifice and offers it to God in the name of all the people. The faithful indeed, by virtue of their royal priesthood, participate in the offering of the Eucharist. They exercise that priesthood, too, by the reception of the sacraments, prayer, and thanksgiving, the witness of a holy life, abnegation, and active charity."[25]

One of the great new aspects of the Church at this most recent Council was the presence of lay observers and observers from other faith traditions. Archbishop Derek Worlock of England, comments here on an eventful moment in this regard:

> "I for one will never forget the morning during the third session of the Council when Patrick Keegan was chosen to address the Fathers in Saint Peter's in the name of the laity. It was allegedly the first time a lay voice had been heard in a General Council of the Church since the days of the Emperor Constantine in A.D.

325. It was certainly one of the high spots in my recollection of Vatican II.[26]

The words of Patrick Keegan to the Council were these:

> "The Lay Apostolate cannot be an isolated entity in the Church. It reaches its fullness in close collaboration with all the other members of the Church. By its very nature it demands a constant and regular exchange between the hierarchy and the laity. It is for us lay people to bring our pastors our experience of the world in which we live, and to seek from them guidance in our endeavor to respond to these needs. In simple terms, there must be "family dialogue" of which our Holy Father, Pope Paul, has spoken so frequently and emphasized in his recent letter Ecclesiam Suam."[27]

You will notice in this one short passage an urgent plea, using words and phrases like "collaboration," "constant and regular exchange," and "family dialogue." If you would return to the first section of this book you will realize why in so many instances what Patrick Keegan was pleading for has not yet been realized in many areas of the Church. To realize this kind of genuine mutuality in mission requires a major conversion and commitment on the part of all those involved. It requires a new way of being with one another in a mutuality of love and service of others, in the name and place of Jesus.

In the conclusion to a talk entitled, "A Last Look at the Council," Yves Congar, O.P., made this statement, which helps to describe how we have been called to "be the Church in a new way." This talk was given at the University of Fribourg in 1979, and later published in the book cited in the Endnotes.

> "The earlier view (of the Church) was dominated until the time of Vatican II by a juridical definition of the Church as a perfect society or a 'complete society' that was unequal and hierarchical. … Vatican II, however, taught an ecclesiology of Christian existence as a Church that is basically sacramental. The vitality of such a Church comes from its base, consisting of people who, filled with enthusiasm for the Gospel, create more or less formal

communities. This encourages not individualism, but a situation of personal choice motivated by deep conviction."[28]

To bring this same concept before us again, I would like to repeat an earlier quotation from Cardinal Avery Dulles found in Part B of this section. In commenting on the <u>Dogmatic Constitution on the Church</u>, he wrote:

> "...the Constitution devotes an entire chapter to the description of the Church as the 'new People of God.' This title, solidly founded in Scripture, met a profound desire of the Council to put greater emphasis on the human and communal side of the Church, rather than on the institutional and hierarchical aspects, which have sometimes been overstressed in the past... While everything said about the 'People of God' as a whole, is applicable to the laity, it should not be forgotten that the term "People of God" refers to the total community of the Church, including the pastors as well as the other faithful."[29]

From my perspective then, the fact that we have been "called to be the Church in a new way" is an exciting and energizing concept. It is really not a break with the past, but a clarification and reordering of the roles of all of the members of the Church. Each member, of whatever rank or position, is called to make God present and visible by being a living example of the Gospel teachings. The laity need the pastors and the pastors need the laity. Although their roles may differ they have a common mission...to make God known and loved and to present themselves to the world as God's People – a Unity of Love.

I would like to take this opportunity to say once more, that the main purpose of this "reflective memoir" is to describe one effort to enable ecclesial groups to grow in their ability to become more and more that kind of living presence as the People of God. We must be more than a collection of individuals. As Church we are called to be One, Holy, Catholic, and Apostolic. Our mission is the evangelization and transformation of a world that knowingly or unknowingly longs for the peace, unity, and love that only God can give through grace and the instrumentality of His living presence on earth.

PART III.
LIGHTHOUSE INTERLUDE
1992-1996

Even though the Lighthouse is not included in the title of this book, I want to present it as another religious symbol on my journey of faith, my journey of life. I assure you that this is not an afterthought, but truly an interlude. A Lighthouse has the purpose of guiding one to a port of safety. On top of Methodist Hospital in Indianapolis, a large Lighthouse stands near the helicopter landing space. I spent seventy-two days in that hospital in 1994, hovering between life and death. With God's help, and that of excellent physicians and nurses, it proved to be a port of safety for me. Now that it is over, I consider it one of the greatest religious experiences of my lifetime. Recovery was gradual. I hold the four-year period of 1992-1996, as the "Lighthouse Interlude" between two major phases of my post-conciliar life in Church ministry. After Vatican Council II and until 1992, my assignments were in some way directed toward helping individuals and groups to answer the call to serious co-responsibility for the life and mission of the Church. During my months of recovery in 1995 and early 1996, I continued this work on a limited basis. Then came, what seemed to me to be a most surprising summons ... thus ending the interlude.

Part III. Lighthouse Interlude

I have often shared with my spiritual director that God is revealed to me in timing. Opportunities, events, and even unexpected and somewhat undesirable happenings seem to surface just at the right time for me. The job description given to me in 1984, as described earlier in this memoir, was brought to its basic completion in the spring of 1992. It was at that time that I began to realize that another "timing event" was about to take place! I chose to share this story as an "interlude" in this memoir because it provided one of the strongest signs of God's providential action in my life.

In April of 1992, I submitted my resignation to the Chancellor of the archdiocese. I knew that I was not in good health, but the symptoms were puzzling to doctors. My legs were numb from the knees down and I was having some trouble in remembering, although that aspect was not serious. The numbness problem caused me to fall down a flight of stairs several times. My energy level was greatly reduced. I knew that I was not capable of maintaining my position beyond that time. My regular physician sent me to a neurologist to see if the cause of the numbness in my legs could be determined. A test was done that had to be sent to California for evaluation. A month passed before the results came back saying that I had to have immediate B-12 shots and have them every day for two weeks. (Ordinarily they are given no more than once a month.) I was diagnosed with a severe B-12 deficiency that had damaged my spinal column and permanently damaged the nerves and muscles in my legs. Gradually the B-12 treatments were put on the regular schedule and I continue to receive them.

In August of 1992, I asked my community for a time of sabbatical, which was really more of a sick-leave. I received the permission with a grateful heart. I spent the scholastic year 1992-1993 at Saint Meinrad School of Theology. I was able to earn seven graduate hours in theology during that time. Being settled in where I could pray, read, and study, without the hassle of city driving and demanding schedules, helped greatly. I did not have to contend with stairs, as elevators were readily available. I continued to check with my doctor. I came through the sabbatical year with no major problems. When I returned to my convent in Indianapolis, I asked if I could set up a small office and work on a project in my field of expertise and experience. I created a brochure advertising my availability for presentations, workshops, and retreats on the topic of "The Spirituality of Groups". For about eight months I was kept moderately busy working with pastoral staffs, school faculties, pastoral councils, religious communities and other groups. This phase of the "Interlude" took place between July of 1993, and April of 1994.

Finally, in April of 1994, I became violently nauseated one night around 9:00 o'clock. I was taken to the hospital where extensive tests were done until around 1:30 a.m. At that time I was told simply, "See you own doctor within the week." When I did that, an endoscopy was done and I was told that I had a cancerous tumor at the junction of my stomach and esophagus. In the introduction to this section of the memoir I called this event "one of the greatest religious experiences of my lifetime." My reason for saying that was that when I learned the nature and seriousness of my condition and the radical means that would be needed to treat it, I was able to maintain a very deep sense of peace. This was a pure gift from God. Without realizing it at the time, I was given the grace to put into practice these words of our foundress, Saint Mother Theodore Guerin: "Put aside all uneasiness about the future. Place yourself gently into the hands of Providence."

When I contacted the member of our General Council to whom I reported, Sister Judith Shanahan (R.I.P.), I was told to contact Judith A. Barrett, a registered nurse practitioner, who was serving as a medical care consultant to the Sisters of Providence at that time. Her role in securing the oncologist and surgeon who treated me was truly a gift of Providence, as were all of the physicians and nurses who cared for me over an extensive period of time. I want to mention in particular, Dr. William M. Dugan, Jr., my oncologist, and Dr. Frank Lloyd, Jr., my surgeon. I had six weeks of chemotherapy and six weeks of radiation therapy. After that, on June 27, 1994, I had surgery to remove the cancerous growth. It was also necessary to remove half of my stomach, the lower third of my esophagus, my spleen and part of my diaphragm. Prior to the surgery Dr. Dugan said to me, "I think you should know that Dr. Lloyd is very well qualified to perform this surgery. He has done post-graduate work in oncology surgery at the Roswell Park Cancer Institute in Buffalo, New York." Judith Barrett, Dr. Dugan and Dr. Lloyd were the human instruments of God's Providence. It was again a singular grace that I could so easily "place myself gently into their hands" at this crucial moment in my life. The day before the surgery, Dr. Lloyd said to me, "I need to tell you that this surgery could go this way or that way." In saying this he held his hand upward and then turned it downward. That was a very gentle way of telling me that I could live or die. I remember having responded to that by saying, "You have to do what you have to do." I did live through the surgery, but there was a very long period of recovery. For most of the time in the hospital, I was lying flat on my back. Every week I was taken to the radiology department for a test to see if the connection between my stomach and esophagus (the anastimosis) was healing. Week after week the answer was, "No." Finally, a thoracic surgeon came into my room. He said, "Sister, we have to do something. You are not healing on the inside. There are five things that we could do." After describing the first one he added, "But that would be fatal." I did not hear two, three, or four. Then when he reached number five he said, "So what we plan to do is to make an incision through your upper back and see if we can go through and pull things together. But we are going to wait one more week." I remember having questioned, "Why one more week?" All he said was, "Just one more week."

Another complication was the development of decubitous ulcers on my posterior as a result of the lengthy time in bed. When the plastic surgeon, working on that aspect of my case, heard that the proposed surgery was to take place through an incision in my upper back, he decided to graft skin from my upper leg onto my lower back at the same time. When the "one more week" had passed, the day arrived for these two surgeries to take place. When the final test was run, Judith Barrett was standing behind me at the head of the table on which I was lying. All of a sudden, I felt her patting both of my cheeks. She said, "It is healed. We don't have to do the surgery!!" Then when the plastic surgeon examined the ulcers, he said, "I have never seen wounds like those heal so fast. We do not have to graft skin." (His exact words!) Thus, two surgeries were cancelled on the same day. Judith, our nurse practitioner, told me later that she felt that I could never have survived those surgeries given my weakened state at that time.

I entered the hospital with the lighthouse atop it on June 27, 1994. It was truly a safe port in a stormy part of my life. I left there on September 7, 1994, recovered and alive but severely debilitated from the ordeal. I would say that it took most of the next year to fully recover. Gradually, I began to continue my work in the formation, development, and renewal of groups with an emphasis on the spirituality of groups and the importance of learning a process approach to change and renewal.

Again, my rationale for including this "Lighthouse Interlude," which is seemingly so unrelated to the general thrust of this memoir, is that it marks a key religious experience in my life, my journey of faith. In those many hours and days and weeks of waiting for recovery, somehow the gentle hands of Providence upheld me. I never thought I would be able to say that I have a deep sense of gratitude for having had an encounter with cancer. It has given me an understanding and perspective on life that I could never have achieved without it. The image that I now have is that my life is about an inch long – even if I live to be 99! On either end of that inch a line extends backward to eternity and forward to eternity. Even now, after fifteen years, I look back upon this experience and find myself filled with gratitude, not just because I have recovered, but more because of having had the experience of God's loving care, strength, and inner peace, in a most profound way.

I began this section by mentioning "timing" as one of the God-signals in my life. As I look back, each new assignment or other major event of my life came at just the right time. And then it happened once again! In May of 1996, I received a letter from our General Superior, Sister Nancy Nolan. I was asked to take on the work of Promoter of the Cause for the canonization of our foundress, then known as Venerable Mother Theodore Guerin, but now known as Saint Mother Theodore Guerin. Another timely and unexpected call! By this time I was fully recovered and ready for the task. The Lighthouse Interlude was a great preparation for what could be the final phase of my journey of faith.

Now we are moving toward the Dome!

PART IV.
DOME
1996 – 2006

Two different assignments in Rome gave me experiences of viewing the Dome of Saint Peter's Basilica as a symbol of the universality of the Church. The Dome is also, for me, a symbol of the "universal call to holiness," which was a key teaching in Chapter Five of the Dogmatic Constitution on the Church. As in the case of the Arch and the Steeples, the Dome is also a symbol of God's abiding presence, and a reminder of the words of Jesus, "I am with you always, even until the end of time." Being present in Saint Peter's Basilica with persons of every race, color, creed, and nationality, is an experience of universality that cannot be learned from a book. Standing in the Square of Saint Peter's in the shadow of the Dome and in the midst of thousands of God's people, is a vivid reminder of the prayer of Jesus, "That they all may be ONE!"

Part IV. Dome (1996-2006)
A. The Purpose of the Church

The theme running through this book, as you have surely discovered by now, (!) is that the teachings of the Second Vatican Council have called all of us to be more vibrantly aware of the fact that we are, together with persons of every rank and position in the Church, the living and breathing Body of Christ, the Church. What that really means, and what that calls each of us to be and to do, can best be learned by a prayerful and studious reading of the two major documents on the Church issuing from the Council.

In reflecting on the purpose of the Church recently, I thought of the time when the disciples of Jesus asked, "Lord, teach us to pray." From my perspective, the response of Jesus gave a wonderful explanation of the purpose of the Church. Beginning with the salutation, "Our Father," Jesus was asking us to pray that all humankind would, in reality, become one family, one body. "Who art in heaven," directs us to our real home. Then after an expression of praise in "hallowed be Thy name," Jesus prayed for the coming of the reign of God, "Thy Kingdom come." That core request in the prayer encapsulates the purpose of the Church. All of us are called to make the reign of God known and experienced by revealing God's love, mercy, and justice in all of our relationships. If these qualities were ever to be fully realized, God's Will would be done, "on earth as it is in heaven." When we pray, "give us this day our daily bread," we are asking that we and all of the members of our common body of humankind will have what is needed and necessary for life. To make this a reality, we are called to collaborate with God in meeting the needs of others. I know that this request for daily bread is also a request for the Eucharistic Bread, the living person of Jesus. I cannot refrain from adding here my favorite insight into the Eucharist. It is from the writings of Saint Peter Chrysologus, but I am unsure of the exact source.

> "Just as two pieces of wax melted together become one, so those who receive Holy Communion become one with Christ, and Christ becomes one with them."

It is not surprising that "the eucharistic sacrifice, the source and summit of the Christian life"[32] should be inherent in the life and purpose of the Church.

Finally, we ask God's forgiveness, according to our measure of forgiving others, and then ask for protection in facing the trials and temptations on the journey of life.

Jesus could so easily and beautifully express in what we now call, "The Lord's Prayer," such a wonderful composite of the purpose of the Church. We are called to be a People, God's presence in the world, not as a haphazard collection of individuals, but as a unity of persons with a common vision and a shared goal – a life of uninterrupted and unending union with God. The real purpose of the Church then, is to lead all of us to heaven. We love and serve God in one another along life's journey.

We are well aware of the fact that the Church goes about its mission of being the presence of Christ in the world in many and varied ways. The pastoral and sacramental ministry of bishops and priests are enabling and fortifying for the members of the Church as they pursue their divine purpose. Other more organized and sometimes institutional efforts to provide education, health care, and social services, have the same goal, to serve and help one another through the vicissitudes of life and to improve the quality of life. All fit the category of pastoral ministry. Hopefully, both the contributors of these works of love and mercy, and those who are the recipients are aware of the faith dimension of these activities. It is hoped, too, that in some way the recipients will also be the contributors when the opportunity presents itself. We are all called to serve one another.

In the more than 2000 years since Jesus called us into being as a Church, there have been men, women, and even some children, whose lives have exemplified a profound and deep understanding of the call of Jesus to lead a life of loving service of God and of one another. In some instances the lives of these persons were examples of heroic love and service. In the early days of the Church, persons such as these were recognized and honored locally and in an informal way. This recognition was a way of reminding the people in the local area of the challenge that is offered to everyone to be holy as God is holy. It was not until the 1200's that the Universal Church began a formal process to identify and to recognize persons whose lives were worthy of our imitation and veneration and to formally declare them "saints." From the mid 1200's to the present day the method used in making these identifications has varied slightly. The most recent articulation of the process for the formal proclamation of sainthood was presented in the 1983 revision of the Code of Canon Law. The actual completion of the process of canonization allows the name of the newly proclaimed saint to be mentioned in the Canon of the Mass. Of course, not every person who has lived a holy and heroic life has been canonized. There are, no doubt, many "unproclaimed" saints in heaven. The Church engages this process as a means of reminding the rest of us of our purpose and goal in life, and to show us examples of persons whose lives can be an inspiration to us as examples of Christian life at its best. Currently, there are three major steps in the process for canonization:

1. There is a thorough examination of the writings, letters, journals, and teachings of the person under consideration for canonization, and testimonies of persons who would have known the person being considered. This documentation is compiled in a ponderous volume called the Positio Super Virtutibus (Statement on Heroic Virtues). When this process is satisfactorily completed, the title "Venerable" is bestowed.

2. For beatification, there is required one example of a miraculous intervention by God after a prayer of intercession was made to the person under consideration. Eight witnesses must testify under oath at a formal investigation held in the Tribunal of the diocese or archdiocese where the miracle occurred. After thorough examination, a formal report is sent to Rome where it is again examined by a panel of physicians and two other panels, one of theologians and another from the Office of the Congregation for the Causes of Saints. When and if these two groups give a positive report, the Postulator then prepares a formal document called Positio Super Miraculo. (Statement on the Miracle) It is presented to the Pope for his review and approval. If the approval is given, plans are begun for the Beatification, at which time the title of "Blessed" is conferred.

3. A second miraculous intervention is required for canonization, and all of the steps followed for the first miracle are required in examining the second one.

After a thorough examination, the second document, the Positio Super Miraculo is prepared and presented to the Holy Father for final approval for canonization. If the approval is given, a special Consistory is called at which the Holy Father announces the names of those to be canonized and the date of the solemn ceremony of canonization is given.

As stated earlier, this extensive process is engaged as a way of reminding all of us that we are called to holiness and to a life with God, a life without end. There are many more persons now enjoying the presence of God whose lives were never so thoroughly examined. From time to time we are given examples of persons whose lives strongly exemplified the universal call to holiness. The events of beatifications and canonizations are simply reminders to all of us of our reason for being. These events are holy reminders of our future life of eternal joy with God and with all whom we know and love.

The processes of beatification and canonization are simply one means of confirming the effectiveness of the "Purpose of the Church," that is, to lead all people to heaven.

In the next section we will learn more about Saint Mother Theodore Guerin, whose process for sainthood I was privileged to have served for eleven years, first as Promoter of the Cause, then as Vice Postulator. Finally and briefly, I served as Director of the Shrine where her remains are now venerated.

Saint Mother Theodore understood, promoted, and lived the mission of the Church. She was truly a woman of the Church.

B. A Universal Home

At this point I would like to share how, in time, this new assignment as Promoter of the Cause for canonization of our Foundress, would put me in touch with Rome and with Vatican City, the Universal Home of the People of God. Before making my first trip to Rome, I spent a year re-examining Mother Theodore's life and works.

I began my work in September of 1996. There was much to learn and to re-learn. From my perspective, her comparatively brief life - only fifty-eight years – was amazingly full and profoundly inspiring. Even though I was very familiar with the life story of Venerable Mother Theodore, it was important for me to study the copious documents so well kept and organized by several previous archivists and general secretaries. I want to mention with gratitude, in particular, Sisters Ann Kathleen Brawley and Eileen Ann Kelley. Of course, all of us hold in high regard the memory of Sister Joseph Eleanor Ryan, who prepared the official document on the heroic virtues of our Foundress. It was a major undertaking and is a ponderous and inspirational volume entitled, "Positio Super Virtutibus, or "Statement on Heroic Virtues". The formal approval of this document allowed Mother Theodore to be given the title Venerable in 1992. In addition to studying the documentation, I discovered very quickly that Mother Theodore had friends and devotees throughout the country and in far-flung parts of the world. This was, no doubt, the result of the way Sisters of Providence have told the founding story for well over a century. Such widespread knowledge had already done much to promote the Cause. There were requests for presentations, both at the Motherhouse and on location across the country. Many visitors came to the tomb of Venerable Mother Theodore. There were requests for presentations to various church groups and schools. Correspondence came from far and wide requesting intercessory prayer and information about the life and good works of Mother Theodore.

After a year of re-orientation, I made my first Roman contact. I introduced myself by letter to the Postulator, Dr. Andrea Ambrosi, who had been appointed to that post by our Congregation in 1994. Dr. Ambrosi was our official representative at the Office of the Congregation for the Causes of Saints. The Cause for the canonization of Mother Theodore had been introduced in 1909, shortly before the beginning of

World War I. A series of world and Church events slowed the process down. One was the primitive means of transportation and communication in the early 1900's. Then two World Wars followed. The Church's involvement with the Second Vatican Council was another cause for interruption. Then, the fact that between 1909 and 1994, ten different Postulators were assigned to the Cause, added another reason for the delay of the process. This last one was the result of Postulators having been made bishops and transferred from Rome. Others had to be replaced because of illnesses, deaths or resignations. But 1994 was a providential year for our Cause. Dr. Ambrosi, a layman and canon lawyer, accepted our Cause. He is a graduate of the Gregorian University in Rome. This was the first Cause that he had taken in the United States. (He now has thirteen other Causes here.) By this time, the materials had been passed from postulator to postulator for almost ninety years. When Dr. Ambrosi received the documentation related to the Cause, he examined it carefully. He read the account of the first reported cure that had taken place in 1908. The formal trial had been conducted in what was then the Diocese of Indianapolis. When Dr. Ambrosi examined the diocesan testimony of the formal witnesses, including medical doctors, he realized that it was worthy of examination by the panel of medical experts appointed by the Congregation for the Causes of Saints. The testimony was approved unanimously by that group. It then was reviewed by a group of theologians and a group of Cardinals. When all of these gave a positive response this was then submitted to Pope John Paul II, who also confirmed the testimony. We received word in the summer of 1997 that we were to prepare for the second step in the process,

1997 — With United States Ambassador to the Vatican, Corrine Boggs

Beatification. The General Superior at that time, Sister Diane Ris, her first assistant, Sister Ann Margaret O'Hara, and another member of the Council, Sister Joan Slobig, went to Rome for the Consistory at which Pope John Paul II announced that the beatification ceremony would be celebrated on October 25, 1998.

In the fall of 1997, I was sent to Rome to begin the remote preparations for the beatification. In the section of this book on "The Widening Circles of Church" I wrote of my first trip to Rome in 1980. At that time I spent one month there on a different assignment, so that was a good preparation for this visit. I had some sense of the city and of the modes of transportation, the currency, and the Italian culture. What made it a very special time was the fact that I was able to be a guest of the Benedictine Sisters of Ferdinand, Indiana, who were on the staff of the North American College located on the Janiculum Hill. Sisters Rebecca Abel, Benedicta Clauss and some years later, Sister Susan Hooks, were gracious and helpful in many ways. It was good to be back among seminarians again. These young men were from dioceses throughout the United States. The North American College (or NAC, as it is often called) is really a residence hall and a House of Priestly Formation. The seminarians are students in various universities throughout the city of Rome. I was again immersed in Benedictine hospitality as I had been at Saint Meinrad, and I was surrounded once more by young men who were preparing to carry on the priestly ministry of the Church. This, too, was another experience of the "widening circles of the Church." But being in Rome was the outer circle. It was truly a Universal Home for me. Strangely enough, I did not have the feeling of being in a foreign city, or in a foreign country.

I can offer here only a few of the responsibilities that were mine during the approximately four weeks spent in Rome in the fall of 1997. A privilege that I had was meeting the Honorable Corrine Boggs, our ambassador to the Vatican. One of the most important tasks was to meet with the Postulator, Dr. Ambrosi, in his office near the Piazza Navona. He had sent his translator, Maria Ponce de Leon, to meet me at the Largo Argentina, where I had arrived by bus from NAC. I found Dr. Ambrosi and Maria to be very gracious and helpful. Even though all of our communications required the services of a translator, we seemed to be able to conduct our affairs with a minimum of difficulty. I learned a variety of details that I needed to attend to as we moved toward the long awaited day of the beatification. I met with a number of persons responsible for various aspects of the ceremony. I was to arrange for about forty priests who would be in our delegation to serve as Eucharistic Ministers. I was asked to have a deacon from our archdiocese to serve in that capacity during the Mass at which the Holy Father would be celebrant. We had one deacon from our archdiocese that year, Deacon Rick Eldred, who is now a pastor. He was very pleased to fill this position. Deacon Rick had been taught by the Sisters of Providence in Terre Haute, Indiana for twelve years! (Did the soon-to-be "Blessed" Mother Theodore plan that??) I was also asked to assign three Mass servers from Indiana. There were two from the Archdiocese of Indianapolis studying in Rome at the time, and one from the Diocese of Gary. They accepted eagerly. Another responsibility was to meet with an official in the Office of Liturgy to discuss the matter of the date of the feast, as a feast day is assigned at the time of the beatification. All I needed to do was to provide information. I was asked (in Italian) the date of Mother Theodore's "first birth." When I shared that it was October 2, that day was not available as it was already the Feast of the Guardian Angels. I was then asked the date of her "second birth" (meaning the date of her death). When I responded that it was May 14, that day was not available either because it was the Feast of Saint Matthew, the Apostle. I was told that the feast would be on October 3, the day after the date of her "first birth." That was very appropriate, since it was also the date of her baptism. God's Providence works in wonderful ways! Another responsibility was to see to the preparation of the reliquary to hold the first class relic that would be presented to the Holy Father during the beatification ceremony. Maria Ponce de Leon had purchased the reliquary for us, but I had to purchase a lining for the floor of the case. I went to a large store in which bolts of material were stacked from floor to ceiling. When I asked for one-fourth of a yard of red transparent velvet, you would have thought that I had asked to purchase the store! The clerk could not have been more polite and helpful. I met with the same courtesy when Maria took me to the Vatican Bank to open an account so that I would be able to take care of my monetary needs during this stay and those of the future. I give these simple accounts in tribute to the kindness of the people I met in "my" Universal Home.

One of the distinct advantages of securing hospitality at the North American College was the fact that I had easy access to means of keeping in touch with Sister Diane Ris, our General Superior at the time. I was able to send her frequent e-mails and fax messages and, of course, to speak with her by phone. Being with English-speaking persons for meals and evening visits was helpful in making me feel at home. One of the greatest blessings was the celebration of the Eucharist in that Universal Home, both at the seminary and also in several different churches of Rome. It was a special grace to be present for the liturgy in Saint Peter's Basilica. The Basilica and the Square in front of it are often filled with persons of every age, race, creed, and nation. We may not yet have achieved the great desire of Jesus, "...that all may be one...," but the spirit one feels in that place leads one to believe, even more strongly, that all things are possible with God. In Chapter Two of the Dogmatic Constitution on the Church we read:

> "The one people of God is accordingly present in all the nations of the earth, since its citizens, who are taken from all nations, are a kingdom whose nature is not earthly but heavenly."[30]

Another passage from this same document extends the concept of God's People in a way that encourages us in our hope for the realization of a full unity.

> "The Church knows that she is joined in many ways to the baptized who are honored by the name of Christian, but who do not however profess the Catholic faith in its entirety or have not preserved unity or communion under the successor of Peter. These Christians are in some real way joined to us in the Holy Spirit, for by his gifts and graces, his sanctifying power is also active in them and he has strengthened some of them even to the shedding of their blood. And so the Spirit stirs up desires and actions in all of Christ's disciples in order that all may be peaceably united, as Christ ordained, in one flock under one Shepherd."[31]

So, if we, as Catholics, want to enable this realization of the prayer of Jesus, "...that all may be one..." we need to present ourselves as a body of believers imbued with the spirit and life of Jesus, the head of our

Mystical Body, the Church. We do this best by our lives and works of love, mercy, and justice. While our true Universal Home is Heaven, our Universal Home here on earth is that cordoned off section of the Italian boot called Vatican City.

C. Woman of the Church

While this is not a biography of Saint Mother Theodore Guerin, I am pleased that in our journey from arch to steeples to dome, her story seems to fit well into this final section. Her missionary life and zeal revealed her understanding of, and commitment to, the universality of the Church. She proved this by her life of dedicated service in building up the Body of Christ, the People of God. This can best be understood by reading her account in The Journals and Letters of Mother Theodore Guerin. I also leave it to some of the books listed in the References at the end of his memoir, to give you specific details of her life from her birth in France in 1798, until her death in America in 1856.

"The Universal Call to Holiness" found in Chapter Five of the Dogmatic Constitution on the Church was realized by Saint Mother Theodore. We read there, "It is therefore quite clear that all Christians in any state or walk in life are called to the fullness of Christian life and to the perfection of love, and by this holiness a more human manner of life is fostered also in earthly society."[33] Mother Theodore's life was a testimony to these words, and so in the place of the Dome, our universal home, this woman of the Church was solemnly recognized as having answered the call to holiness.

At this time I would like to share what I consider to be her legacy to us, as her co-members in the Church. The legacy of Mother Theodore is not a material or a monetary one. It is a spiritual gift bestowed on her by the Holy Spirit. This kind of legacy is sometimes referred to as a charism, a gift unique to the person to whom it is given, but given not just for the sake of that person. It is for a larger good and purpose. Sometimes the charism is so strong and vibrant, that it lives on over the years, or decades, or even centuries in other people, who have been drawn to that gift of the Spirit given to the original recipient. So how might we define this unusual gift, this charism of the Spirit as it is found in the life of Saint Mother Theodore Guerin. I am sure it defies full description, but we might begin to describe it in this way: **a profound trust in God's Providence.** Five major themes seem to reveal themselves in her living of her charism.

First of all, she was rooted and grounded in a strong faith in God. Faith is different from, and more than, simple belief. Faith implies trust in the God who loves you. It was this trust, which sustained the young Anne Therese Guerin from her earliest years of a difficult childhood. While still very young she had to assume major responsibilities for her family. Her fidelity to her family developed into a sense of community with God's People, and to a desire to respond in love to those in need.

Secondly, the poverty and simplicity of her home life, coupled with a series of family tragedies, taught her early on, "to cast her cares upon the Lord," and to find that God was her strength in the face of any difficulty.

The third theme, I believe, is that her awareness of the needs of the world around her played an important part in her responding to the call to religious life. Her great heart had need of reaching beyond itself, beyond her immediate family, to a France bruised and broken by the recent Revolution, and eventually, to an America in its early stages of development and growth in the faith.

In the fourth theme, Mother Theodore, in her comparatively short life at Saint Mary-of-the-Woods - just sixteen years - showed an indomitable spirit of perseverance in the face of almost insurmountable odds. She was a woman of courage so strong, that one can only wonder at her amazing accomplishments in spite of grave illnesses, painful misunderstandings, and a dire lack of resources for the work to be done. She faced all of these with a capacity for risk-taking and surrender to God's action in her life that is truly the mark of saintliness. More that that, she endured these trials with a joyful spirit and as she, herself, once said, "...a spirit of natural gaiety."

Finally, in addition to her life of faith, or rather supportive of that life, she nurtured a deep devotional life. Her Eucharistic life was revealed in her earnest desire to celebrate this unique presence of God. Her warm and loving devotion to Mary, the Mother of God, can be found in many of her writings and in the memoirs of those who knew her best in life. Having been born on the Feast of the Guardian Angels, she frequently re- minded the sisters to invoke the help of these heavenly spirits in their work with the children. Jesus' saving act of redemption on the Cross was central to the spiritual life of Saint Mother Theodore, as it is for all of us as Christians. She certainly did not have a morbid attachment to suffering, but she embraced the cross with courage when it presented itself in her life. She always saw the cross as a special sign of God's favor. While she may not have liked the crosses that came, she saw these sufferings as redemptive and so could receive them with grace, knowing as she said, "It is the way to heaven."

This brief account of the spiritual life of Saint Mother Theodore Guerin is a foundation for a more profound explanation of her spirituality as a "Woman of the Church." As I read what I believe many declare to be the core document of the Second Vatican Council, "Lumen Gentium," or the "Dogmatic Constitution on the Church," I had a new insight. My insight from reading that document of Vatican II was, that even though Saint Mother Theodore died more than one hundred years before the opening of that Council, she had within herself the profound spirit of Church and the great wisdom hidden in that document. I am willing to admit that this is my bias, but here I present my rationale.

Since a major theme of this book has been the Church as defined by the most recent Council, I would like to begin by listing in summary fashion the descriptions of the Church as given in "Lumen Gentium," the Light of Humanity. As I do this, I think of what these phrases might have meant to Saint Mother Theodore Guerin, had she seen them gathered into one formal Church document. I tend to believe that these words would have intensified her already great love for the Church. I believe that, in her person, she exemplified many of the terms in her works of love, mercy, and justice among God's People. And so we read that the Church is:

- "a sign and instrument of communion with God and of unity among all persons
- a sacrament of salvation
- a people brought into unity from the unity of the Father, the Son, and the Holy Spirit
- the seed and the beginning of the Kingdom of Christ and of God
- a sheepfold - the sole and necessary gateway to which is Christ
- a flock of which God is Shepherd
- a cultivated field – the tillage of God
- a choice vineyard planted by the heavenly cultivator
- the building of God
- the household of God in the Spirit
- the dwelling place of God among all humankind

- the holy temple – compared to the holy city, the New Jerusalem
- a communion of life, love, and truth
- our mother
- spotless spouse of the spotless lamb
- mystically constituted Body of Christ
- a community of faith
- a People of God
- a Mystery"[34]

Without having had the advantage of this powerful Church teaching, and without having had formal theological education, I believe that Saint Mother Theodore held these truths within her heart. This is what enabled her to leave her beloved France for an unknown part of the world, knowing that she would continue to be a part of the People of God and to build up the Body of Christ in another part of the Universal Church of which she was a vibrant member. She literally laid down her life for her faith, since she accepted the assignment to the frontier of Mid-America in a state of poor health. In spite of that, in only sixteen years, she established the Congregation of the Sisters of Providence of Saint Mary-of-the-Woods; Saint Mary's Female Institute, the forerunner of Saint Mary-of-the-Woods College, and sixteen other schools. She also founded several orphanages and a free pharmacy. Mother Theodore joined the other sisters in caring for the sick poor in the area. All if these good works, imbued as they were with her depth of spirituality, certainly make her worthy of the title, "Woman of the Church."

While the models of the Church given in the foregoing list refer specifically to the Universal Church, I believe that it was the desire and the goal of Saint Mother Theodore that these same qualities would characterize the community that she was called to bring into existence. Some stand out in particular for a newly forming Christian community:

+ a community of faith
+ a household of God
+ a communion of life, love and truth
+ a flock of which God is Shepherd
+ mystically constituted Body of Christ
+ a People of God

Mother Theodore realized that Jesus is present in the Church in all of its parts, in individuals as well as in families, religious communities, and other ecclesial entities. Her sanctity was recognized in the way she revealed that Christian presence in her own person and in the ways she called and inspired others to do the same. On October 15, 1998, Mother Theodore was declared "Blessed" by Pope John Paul II. During that ceremony our Holy Father honored her by saying, "Her life was a perfect blend of humanness and holiness." That is the ultimate compliment!

Saint Mother Theodore Guerin
1798 —1856
Canonized October 15, 2006

D. Celebrating with the World

Before we move to the celebration, we will examine briefly how it came to be, that on a beautiful day in October of 2006, the Dome of Saint Peter's Basilica towered over a crowd of thousands celebrating the canonizations of four persons. One of them was Saint Mother Theodore Guerin, foundress of the Sisters of Providence of Saint Mary-of-the-Woods, Indiana.

In 1839, the Servant of God, Bishop Simon Gabriel Bruté, first bishop of Vincennes, Indiana, sent his vicar- general, Father Celestine de la Hailandiére, to France, in search of a group of sisters to teach the children of his diocese. In 1840, Sister Theodore Guerin and her five sister companions came to Indiana from their motherhouse in Ruillé-sur Loir, France, in the Diocese of Rennes. The Sisters of Providence had been established there in 1806, so only thirty-four years after their foundation these sisters sent six of their members to open their first foreign mission. Because of primitive travel and communication it was deemed necessary for the American community to become independent. However, both communities have retained strong filial ties. For sixteen years Mother Theodore led her small community in service. She led with determination, courage, and kindness, in spite of many physical hardships, as well as grievous misunderstandings with the local bishop. After her death in 1856, the sisters and the people whom Mother Theodore had served, continued to speak lovingly and with gratitude of her care and service. Her compassionate and understanding presence was a gift beyond measure to the people of the frontier. Mother Theodore had given herself completely to the sisters and to her mission to the people, holding nothing back. The words of praise rang loud and clear and seemed never to die out.

In 1878, when the Diocese of Vincennes was moved to Indianapolis, the people continued to tell the newly appointed bishop about her holy and heroic life. Most Reverend Francis Silas Chatard encouraged the Sisters of Providence to have one of their members write the story of the life of Mother Theodore. This biography was written over a three-year period and was completed in 1904, by Sister Mary Theodosia Mug. After the Bishop read the biography, he requested in 1907, that Mother Theodore's body be exhumed and examined. By this time she had been deceased for fifty-one years. The bishop knew that in some instances, God had preserved the bodies or some parts of the bodies of holy persons. When the body was exhumed, the brain was found to be perfectly intact. Bishop Chatard was a medical doctor before he became a priest. He had graduated from the University of Maryland Medical School in 1854. He requested that three doctors examine the brain. One of the doctors was not to be a Catholic. In the report it was stated: "This is a highly unusual phenomenon. The brain is the most delicate tissue in the human body and normally disintegrates within six hours after death." The examining doctors went on to give the size, the weight, the color and the texture of the brain, stating that it looked as if it had just been taken from a living body. The doctor who wrote the final report stated, "There will be those who will say that the brain was preserved because of minerals in the water in the ground. This could not be true, as no other tissue was preserved." (This report is available in the Archives of the Sisters of Providence.)

It is interesting to note that Sister Mary Theodosia, the first biographer of Mother Theodore in 1904, was the recipient of an amazing cure in 1908. On July 11, 1909, Bishop Chatard introduced the Cause for canonization in Rome. Sister Mary Theodosia's cure was later proven to have been miraculous, clearing the path to beatification. A brief description of this cure follows.

Sister Mary Theodosia had been diagnosed with schirrous carcinoma, a severe form of breast cancer, and had had a radical mastectomy in 1906. The primitive surgery at that time damaged all the nerves and muscles in her left arm, so that it was rigid at her side. In

1998 — Introducing Mother Theodore to the throngs in St. Peter's Square on the day of the Beatification

addition, she had an inoperable abdominal tumor. In October of 1908, she was praying for another sister at the tomb of Mother Theodore. The next morning, she found herself to be the one healed! Her arm, which had been rigid for twenty months, was perfectly normal. The abdominal tumor was gone. She was forty-eight years old at the time of the cure and she lived to be eighty-three. She died of arteriosclerosis. The formal trial concerning the miraculous healing was conducted in the then Diocese of Indianapolis. This required the formal testimony of doctors and other witnesses.

After many years of delay caused by a series of church and world events, this case was formally and unanimously approved at the Congregation for the Causes of Saints in Rome. Word of the approval was received at Saint Mary-of-the-Woods in the summer of 1997. On October 15, 1998, Venerable Mother Theodore was beatified and was given the title, "Blessed." We were then moving toward the final step. One more sign from God was needed – one more miracle proven to have occurred after praying through the intercession of Blessed Mother Theodore. This miracle had to be one that had occurred after the beatification, that is, after October 15, 1998.

In the new millennium God granted this favor. Philip McCord, at that time the Facilities Manager for the properties of the Sisters of Providence at Saint Mary-of-the-Woods, was the recipient. Phil had had cataract surgery on both eyes. The first eye healed quickly and completely. After surgery on the second eye, it began to swell, droop, was red, and painful all of the time. Phil could not see out of that eye. He went back to his regular surgeon ten times for treatment and was finally sent to a specialist in another city. The specialist told Phil that he needed a cornea transplant, but given the condition of his eye at that point, it would be a very risky surgery. There was a possibility that he could lose the sight in that eye. After discussing the matter with his wife, who is a registered nurse, they decided to wait. Phil told me that after waiting two months, he was becoming very distressed and depressed. One day he was walking down the inside corridor near our conventual church and heard someone practicing on the organ. He stopped and said to himself, "Maybe I should pray." Then he said, again to himself, "But I am not a Catholic. I don't belong to any church." However, he entered the church and went to one of the pews. He said, "Mother Theodore, this is your house, and I am one of your servants." Then he said he corrected himself and said, "No, I am more like one of your family. If you can help me I would really appreciate it, but if you can't that's O.K." Then he said the first thing that happened was that he had a great feeling of peacefulness and he hadn't had any peace for over two months. He said to himself, "I can live with this if I have to." He went home and didn't mention his visit to the church. However, the next morning when he went into the bathroom and looked into the mirror, his eye was not red, not swollen, not drooping, and there was no pain. He could see, but not clearly. He went back to the specialist. After an examination the doctor said, "Have you seen your own surgeon since you were here last?" When Phil answered in the negative, the doctor then questioned, "Then what did you do?" Phil answered, "I prayed." The doctor said, "You do not need a cornea transplant." The doctor removed a small piece of scar tissue and Phil now has 20/20 vision after having worn glasses from the age of six. The follow-up to this case included the transcription of fifty-five pages of medical documents. We then had to obtain the services of two doctors who had to examine Phil and testify under oath regarding their findings in the presence of two priests who were serving as Vicar Judicial, Monsignor Fred Easton, JCL and Promoter of Justice, Father James Bonke, JCL. A physician and a notary public were the other two members of the examining board. In addition, eight other witnesses had to testify before the same four persons at the Metropolitan Tribunal in Indianapolis. This examination is always held in the Tribunal of the diocese or archdiocese in which the cure took place. When that phase was completed, the testimony was translated into Italian. It was wrapped and sealed with hot wax and the Archbishop's seal. It was then taken to the Apostolic Nuncio in Washington, D.C. Being a diplomat, the Nuncio could get it through customs without having it opened. I received notification on June 7, 2003, that the testimony had arrived in Rome, and that all of the procedures had been followed accurately. But that was not the end. Another medical panel in Rome, a panel of theologians, and another of Cardinals from the Office of the Congregation for the Causes of Saints had to review and approve the testimony. Finally, in mid-February of 2006, we received word that all three groups had given positive approval in their reports to the Holy Father. We were told that the canonization would take place in the autumn of 2006. Later we were invited to have representatives at the Consistory at which the date of canonization would be announced. Because of our being in General Chapter, a very important community meeting, our General Superior, Sister Ann Margaret O'Hara, was unable to make the trip to Rome. Sister Mary Ann Phelan, a former assistant in the Office for the Cause, and I attended the Consistory during which Pope Benedict XVI announced the date of canonization to be October 15, 2006.

Over the last eleven years, as I have spoken with many individuals and groups, I have always reminded them that the miracles are not the most important aspect of the process of a person's being named a saint. These signs are interesting, inspiring and intriguing, but the heart of the matter is the way the person has lived a life of heroic sanctity in the love and service of God and God's people. It is important to remember that the saints have only intercessory power with God. Only God works miracles. The accounts of miracles are reminders to us of the power of intercessory prayer and of the goodness and power of God. After thorough examination, miracles are recognized as God's approval of the person whose formal canonization is being sought.

Another important fact to remember is, that God did not create just some people to be saints. By presenting us with so many examples of saints, the Church never lets us forget the universal call to holiness and each one's personal call.

The study and review of Mother Theodore's life, journals, letters, conferences, and the witness of those who knew her in life, was a purely human effort, and therefore subject to human error, no matter how carefully done. That is why the two miracles are required in the process for canonization. These thoroughly examined cases are recognized as a kind of affirmation from God, that this person's life is worthy of our veneration and imitation.

So having fulfilled all of the lengthy tasks that are required in the process of a declaration of sainthood, we were more than ready to share the joy of celebrating with the world! As planned, this celebration took place in Saint Peter's Square on October 15, 2006.

The pilgrims honoring Saint Mother Theodore included the Archbishop of Indianapolis and the four other bishops of Indiana. The bishop of Saint Mother Theodore's home diocese of Saint Brieuc, France, was also present. Of course, many Sisters of Providence from both communities of which Saint Mother Theodore had been a member, were represented. Numerous bishops, priests, religious of other communities, and lay people were there in great numbers, many of whom were former students of the Sisters of Providence. We found ourselves in the midst of the People of God, the Church Universal. Had we had the opportunity to take role call, I feel confident that almost every continent was represented and many different nations, races, and religious beliefs, as well. It was truly a celebration with the world!

As the actual celebration began on a beautiful autumn day, Saint Peter's Square was filled, not only with joyful people, but with the beauty of the solemn liturgical rites of the Church. The backdrop was the façade of Saint Peter's Basilica on which hung large pictures of the four candidates for canonization. At the time of beatification these pictures had been covered with a silk cloth, which was raised as the names were called for beatification. On this day, however, the pictures were uncovered from the beginning of the celebration. The actual ceremony of canonization took place before the Eucharistic liturgy. The Holy Father, Pope Benedict XVI, read a brief account of each person's life of holiness and service to the Church. In his statement on Saint Mother Theodore he said in part:

> "Mother Guerin is a beautiful spiritual figure and a model of Christian life. She was always ready for what the missions of the Church asked of her, finding the strength and courage to put them into effect in the Eucharist, prayer, and an infinite trust in Divine Providence. Her interior strength gave her a particular concern for the poor, and especially for children."

2006 — A special moment at the Canonization Ceremony

Pope Benedict then recalled the words used by Mother Theodore shortly before her death: "How much good has been accomplished by the Sisters of Providence of Saint Mary-of-the-Woods! How much more good they will be able to do if they remain faithful to their holy vocation!"

After the formal proclamations of canonization were made, each of the four delegations sent three or four representatives to make presentations to the Holy Father. Our group was made up of Sister Denise Wilkinson, General Superior; Philip McCord, recipient of the second miraculous cure; and this writer, the Vice Postulator and Promoter of the Cause.

2006 — Pope Benedict XVI at the Canonization with our Postulator Dr. Avv. Andrea Ambrosi

Sister Denise carried the chalice that would be used during the Mass. I carried the paten with host and purificator, and Philip McCord carried a small tray with a gift for the Holy Father. It was truly a wonderful experience to be a part of that entourage. Pope Benedict XVI has a quality of personal presence that exudes peace and kindness.

Being among that throng on such a momentous occasion for our Congregation is a never-to-be-forgotten moment. It was truly the crowning moment of the many years of my life, but especially of the key years covered in this reflective memoir, 1972-2006. Those years of my life helped me in unforeseen ways to grow in my understanding of and love for the Church. From teacher during the years of Vatican II, to Provincial Councillor during the transition years after the Vatican Council, to a member of the Cor Unum Renewal Team, to a staff member of the Center for Planned Change, to Spiritual Director and teacher in a seminary, to Director of an Office for Pastoral Councils, to Promoter for the Cause and Vice Postulator, I found myself, from step to step, more immersed in and identified with the Church.

I recall now the domestic Church of the Tighe Family, where I was first taken to the font of life at Baptism and then taught to live the

Christian life in community. I was called by God in a subtle way to the Sisters of Providence, where my circle of family and Church was widened and deepened. I made an adult promise to a vowed life. My vows were made to God, but they are lived out in communion with my sisters. I want to thank my Community for the encouragement, time, space, and opportunity to share these reflections. I hope that the unexpected and unsought adventures described herein, will somehow reach young women eager to devote themselves to God and the Church in religious life. I invite you to check out the website, www.sistersofprovidence.org and learn about the Sisters of Providence today. If anyone reading this book knows a young woman who seems to share the spirit, courage, vision and trust in Providence that characterized Saint Mother Theodore Guerin, please ask her to contact us.

And now it is time for the final blessing to all who have persevered to the end of this reflective memoir.

May the God of Providence bless you. May you grow each day in your awareness of your union with Jesus, and with all of the members of the Mystical Body of Christ, the Church. May you be a sign and an instrument of God's love, peace and justice to all whom you meet.

2007 — Dedication of the statue of Saint Mother Theodore Guerin at the National Shrine of the Immaculate Conception in Washington D.C. (Teresa Clark, artist – sculptor)

Epilogue

As I come to the end of these reflections on the last forty years and more, I am not under the illusion that "all is well" with the Church. Neither am I discouraged at what remains to be done. What gives me a sense of gratitude and hope is that renewal is an ongoing process. I am pleased that the greater part of my life has been spent in enabling many individuals and groups to pause, to reflect, to choose, and to act, in ways that authenticate themselves as Church, the living Mystical Body of Christ. Life is the most important journey any of us will ever take. Inevitably, we are on this journey of faith with others. We are not traveling the road alone. The ideal is that each group of which we are members will be united as ONE. In the world we speak of the United Nations - a hope, not yet a reality. In the Church we pray, "...that all may be one..." – a hope, not yet a reality. In families and communities we try to be of one mind and one heart, – a hope, not always a reality. This unity can be attained only with God's help united to our selfless and mutual efforts. We are all on a journey of faith, a journey called life. Let us walk with each other in faith, and with God as our Center.

The year 2007 was a time to ruminate, relish, and rejoice. While the contents or this memoir have been gathering in my mind and heart for many years, it was during 2007 that my desire to share my experiences began to be felt very strongly. My community gave me a three months' mini-sabbatical that was spent at Saint Meinrad Seminary. That gave me the time and a familiar space, as well as a prayerful atmosphere, to stop, to consider, and to begin to gather my thoughts at this senior moment in my life! Finally, in 2009, this is completed in time to dedicate it to my parents for their 100th wedding anniversary!

So now you know why "Arch, Steeples, and Dome" have been strong religious symbols for me as I followed a journey of faith, unplanned by me but laid out for me by the teachings of the most significant Council of the Church. This book is certainly not a theological dissertation, nor does it even approach the word, "scholarly." It is an account of a lengthy and rich personal journey, one that I wanted to share before the end of my life here. With all of that said, I look forward to the future with a smile, knowing that my loving God and the Blessed Mother, as well as many loving family and community members are waiting for my arrival in our heavenly home. Once more, I am following the warm advice of our Foundress, Saint Mother Theodore Guerin who wrote: "Put aside all uneasiness about the future. Place yourself gently into the hands of Providence."

I want to end by thanking the hundreds of persons and groups with whom I have pursued the vision of the Second Vatican Council and the Mission of the Church. Through your faith, your commitment, and your willingness to engage a process of corporate renewal, you have helped me to come to a deeper understanding of what it means to be a member of the living Body of Christ, the Church.

Endnotes

1. John O'Malley and others, *Vatican II: Did Anything Happen?* (New York: Continuum, 2007).

2. John O'Malley, *What Happened at Vatican II?* (Cambridge: Belknap Harvard, 2008).

3. Timothy Radcliffe, "The Shape of the Church to Come." *America Magazine*, Vol. 200, April 13, (2009): 21.

4. Alberic Stacpoole, ed., *Vatican II Revisited by Those Who Were There*, (Minneapolis: Winton Press, 1986), xiv-xv.

5. Karl Rahner, *The Church After the Council*, (New York: Herder and Herder, 1966) 17-18.

6. Austin Flannery, ed., *Vatican Council II, The Conciliar and Post Conciliar Documents, Decree on the Up-to-Date Renewal of Religious Life.* 8th ed. (New York: Costello Publishing, 1987) Article 2, 612.

7. Flannery, *Renewal of Religious Life*, Article 4, 613.

8. Flannery, *Renewal of Religious Life*, Article 4, 613.

9. Rahner, 28-29.

10. Freed Bales, *Symlog: The Systemic Multi-Level Observation of Groups.* (Cambridge, Harvard University Press, 1979)

11. *The New American Bible.* (Nashville: Catholic Bible Press, 1969) Ephesians 4:15-16, 1333.

12. *The New American Bible.* Corinthians 12:21, 1296.

13. *Deanery Pastoral Council Guidelines* (Indianapolis: Archdiocese of Indianapolis 1991) 9-10.

14. Avery Dulles, *Documents of Vatican II, Dogmatic Constitution on the Church:* Walter M. Abbott, ed, 24-25.

15. Reuel Howe, *The Miracle of Dialogue.* (New York: Seabury Press, 1663), 3.

16. Flannery, ed., *The Dogmatic Constitution on the Church*, quoting Leo XIII, Encycl. *Satis Cognitum*, 357.

17. Walter Abbott *The Documents of Vatican II*. Pope John XXIII, *Opening Speech for Vatican Council II*, (New York: Herder and Herder, 1966), 715.

18. Abbott, 716.

19. Abbott, 715.

20. Abbott, 715

21. Flannery, *Dogmatic Constitution on the Church*, Chapter 1, Article 7, 355.

22. Flannery, *Dogmatic Constitution on the Church*, Chapter 5, Article 40, 397.

23. Flannery, *Dogmatic Constitution on the Church*, Chapter 2, Article 13, 364.

24. Flannery, *Constitution on the Sacred Liturgy, Introduction*, Chapter 1, 1

25. Flannery, *Dogmatic Constitution on the Church*, Chapter 2, Article 10, 361.

26. Stacpoole, 248.

27. Stacpoole, 248-49.

28. Yves Congar, "A Last Look at the Council." in *Vatican II Revisited by Those Who Were There*, ed., Stacpoole (Minneapolis: Winston Press, 1985). 352-53.

29. Dulles, 24-26.

30. Flannery, *The Dogmatic Constitution on the Church*. Chapter 2, Article 13, 364.

31. Flannery, *The Dogmatic Constitution on the Church*. Chapter 2 Article 15, 366-67.

32. Flannery, *The Dogmatic Constitution on the Church*. Chapter 2, Article 11, 362.

33. Flannery, *The Dogmatic Constitution on the Church*. Chapter 5, Article 40, 397.

34. Flannery, *The Dogmatic Constitution on the Church*. Chapters 1 and 2.

Suggested References and Readings

Abbott, Walter M., S.J., Editor: *The Documents of Vatican II*. New York: Herder and Herder, 1966.

Brown, Mary Borromeo, S.P., *History of the Sisters of Providence of Saint Mary-of-the-Woods. Vol. I.* New York: Benzinger, 1949.

Burton, Katherine, Foreword and Afterword by Mary K. Doyle: *The Eighth American Saint*. Skokie, IL: ACTA Publications, 2007.

Canon Law Society of Great Britain and Ireland in association with The Canon Law Society of Australia and New Zealand and the Canadian Canon Law Society: *The Code of Canon Law*. London: Collins, 1983.

Doyle, Mary K., *Seven Principles of Sainthood, Following Saint Mother Theodore Guerin*. Skokie, IL: ACTA Publications, 2008.

Dulles, Avery, S.J., *A Church to Believe In: Discipleship and the Dynamics of Freedom*. New York: Crossroad, 1982.

Dulles, Avery, S.J., *The Dimensions of the Church*. Woodstock Papers 8. New York: Newman Press, 1967.

Dulles, Avery, S.J., *Models of the Church*. Garden City, New York: Doubleday & Company, Inc., 1974.

Durkin, Mary Cabrini, CSU, in collaboration with Marie Kevin Tighe, S.P. *Trusting Providence*. Kehlerdruck, Germany: Editions du Signe, 2006.

Gilsdorf, Richard W., Edited by Patrick F. Beno. *The Signs of the Times: Understanding the Church Since Vatican II*. Green Bay, WI: Star of the Bay Press, 2008.

Logan, Eugenia, S.P., *History of the Sisters of Providence of Saint Mary-of-the-Woods. Vol. II*. Terre Haute, IN: Moore-Langen, 1978.

Madden, Mary Roger, S.P., *The Path Marked Out: History of the Sisters of Providence of Saint Mary-of-the-Woods. Volume III*. Terre Haute, IN: United Graphics, 1998.

Mitchell, Penny Blaker, *A Woman for Our Time*. Matoon, IL: United Graphics, 1998.

Mitchell, Penny Blaker, *A Woman for All Time*. Indianapolis: Jackson Press, 2006.

McBrien, Richard P., *The Church: The Evolution of Catholicism*. New York: Harper Collins Publishers, 2008.

Mug, Mary Theodosia, S.P., *Life and Life-Work of Mother Theodore Guerin*. New York: Benziger Brothers, 1904.

O'Malley, John W., Stephen Schloesser, Joseph Komonchak, Neil J. Ormerod. Edited by David G. Schultenover. *Did Anything Happen at Vatican II?* New York: Continuum, 2007.

O'Malley, John W., *What Happened at Vatican II?* Cambridge: The Belknap Press of Harvard University, 2008.

Staacpoole, Don Alberic, OSB, Editor, *Vatican II Revisited by Those Who Were There*. Minneapolis, MN: Winston Press, 1986.

Wuthnow, Robert, *Christianity in the 21st Century: Reflections on the Challenges Ahead*. New York: Oxford University Press, 1993.

Young, Julie, *A Belief in Providence: A Life of Saint Theodore Guerin*. Indianapolis: Indiana Historical Society Press, 2007.

Acknowledgements:

Cover: Pam Lynch

Technical Assistance: Juanita Crouch

Kathleen Fleming

I would like to express my sincere gratitude to each person listed above. Your generous gifts of time and talent were essential to this book becoming a reality. I am indebted beyond measure to each one of you for your willing and joyful assistance. My prayerful gratitude will be with you forever.

To Pam, for her artistic ability in capturing in the cover of this book the beauty of the symbols that are so expressive of my memoir.

To Juanita, for her tireless efforts in providing her astute technical assistance needed to deliver the manuscript and photos in good form.

To Kathleen, for her years of dedicated volunteer service in the days prior to the canonization and thereafter, and for her assistance with some of the documentation needed for this book.

Gratefully,
Sister Marie Kevin